WINNING IS FOR LOSERS!

How to use Positive Thinking and the Gift of Fear to Succeed in Life, Love and Business

DEANTE YOUNG

Copyright © 2021 Dirty Truth Publishing. All Right Reserved.

No part of this publication may be reproduced, distributed, or transmitted in any form or by any means, including photocopying, recording, or other electronic or mechanical methods, or by any information storage and retrieval system without the prior written permission of the publisher, except in the case of very brief quotations embodied in critical reviews and certain other noncommercial uses permitted by copyright law.

ISBN: 978-1-7369466-2-6

> To: KP, The most awesome and cool fitness trainer in the land. Your support is phenomenal!
>
> —D.Y.
>
> 10.23.21

Dedicated to Billie Jo. Your support and love inspired the vision for this book. Unlimited gratitude.

—D.Y.

TABLE OF CONTENTS

Introduction 1

Part I: Your Thinking Sucks. Let's Fix It 5
   1. Newsflash: You're a Coward 7
   2. Appropriate Fear is a Gift 13
   3. For the Record, You're a Spoiled Ass Brat 19
   4. If You Knew You Were Gonna Fail, What Would You Do? 25
   5. The 90% Rule: My Positive Energy Formula 31

Part II: Legendary Tales of The Illusion of Failure 35
   6. Michael Jordan Will Never Win a Championship 37
   7. Eminem Will Never Make it as a Rapper 45
   8. Oprah Winfrey Will Never Make It in Television 49

Part III: How to Win 100% of the Time 51
   9. SIMON ARIAS: There's No Success Without Adversity 55
   10. JULIUS CHISHOLM: If You're Not Fighting, You're Being Killed 63
   11. JONATHAN CHURCH: Suffer Today So We Can Conquer Tomorrow 73
   12. HONORÉE CORDER: There's Always a Way if You're Committed 79
   13. ASA COX: There's No Such Word as No 85
   14. WAYNE DAWSON: The Seeds of Greatness Are Within You 89
   15. EMIL GAMIDOV: Failure is Fake 99

16. AARON GREEN: Tomorrow Starts Today 107
17. MARCEL HORSLEY Fear is Afraid of You 113
18. BASHEER JONES: Passion 123
19. MARY JO MILLER: Fearless 127
20. ALLISON OCCKIAL: You Can't Win Unless You Play 133
21. MATTHEW PARKS: Preaching is Easy. Practicing is Hard 141
22. ERIC SEAN: From the Flames We Rise 151
23. JAMES SURACE: Walking in Power 163
24. HALA TAHA: Rejection is Redirection 175
25. MICHAEL VASU: Sacrifice Creates Opportunity 183
26. JOHN WRIGHT: The Wright Way is Your Wright Solution 193
27. DEANTÈ YOUNG: One Monkey Don't Stop No Show 197
Closing Thoughts 205
THE END **207**

Introduction

I was a mediocre little bitch when I started writing this book. I hesitated to reach out to many high-profile people to participate for the same reason that Bill Cosby drugged women.

I didn't want to be told "No."

That's my dirty truth, and it's been yours too often. Charlie Sheen once said that "can't" is the cancer of "happen," which means we are riddled with an incurable disease that forces us to avoid going after what we want in life.

But that's a goddamn lie because the "cancerous can't" is very curable. I've already confronted *myself* for not having the guts to try all types of awesome shit in my life. Now you need to check yourself on your BS.

Failing, losing, and being told "no" freaks you out like a hand on your shoulder in an empty room. It feels like the end of the world, right? Rejection sucks, and the embarrassment it causes makes you feel more uncomfortable than having a rock in your shoe. Why would you want to go through that?

Because "trying" is the only road filled with endless possibilities! Every man-made thing you like is possible because the creators never gave up until their vision was reality.

Think about all the "failing" and "losing" you've experienced in your life so far. Falling off your bike, skinning your knees, making bad grades in school, being rejected by boys who didn't like you, girls laughing in your face, hitting the cones during driver's ed, not filling out an application correctly, making a wrong turn on a road trip, spilling food or drinks on the floor, relationship breakups...you get the idea.

Through all of that imperfection and failing to meet expectations, you learned something new or gained important knowledge that made you better. Falling off your bike resulted in learning how to ride a bike, making a wrong turn allowed you to discover the proper route, and breakups provided the catalyst to correct course and show up better in your next relationship.

You're so worried about a bad outcome that you don't give yourself a chance for a good one. Get over that shit and prevent regret by jumping in and doing the damn thing!

Winning is For Losers! is my third book this year (in a five-month period), and it is one of the best pieces of evidence that I'm worth listening to on this topic. There was a ton of self-doubt in my soul that I could convince elite performers in business, entertainment, and fitness to sit for an interview.

Emil Gamidov, a very driven entrepreneur who owns nearly a dozen fitness clubs, was a man I had never met in person before this project. I admired his drive and mindset, but was convinced he would turn me down.

I came close to not asking him, but I remembered the title of this book I was writing, so I asked him, and he gave me a resounding "Yes!" I was also fearful that James Surace, an internationally known business tycoon, would turn me down, but I asked his wonderful wife Nancy to help the cause, and he said, "Yes!"

My qualifications aside, the eighteen men and women who each have a chapter in this book provide billion-dollar advice by sharing a wealth of their experiences and endless challenges. They are massively committed to excellence in their lives, and all share a common trait that contributes to their enormous success: they ignore the doubts in their head and take consistent action!

Reading this book will help you:

- Gain fulfillment from trying and doing

- Feel more alive by taking chances

- Realize the power and benefit of rejection

- Understand that you will likely feel deflated in the short-term, but can gain fearlessness in the long-term

- Become a much better resource in the lives of others

- And much more!

The incredible possibilities that can come your way if you throw a jab at the face of fear and start trying to do awesome shit are truly endless. Check out Amazon.com and search "Deantè Young in books." Focus on the release date of each one and let that inspire you to ignore the possibility of failing and take action.

Research the astounding achievements and philanthropy of James Surace or read one of Honorée Corder's 53 bestselling books. Have a life-changing conversation with Julius Chisholm, Michael Vasu or Eric Sean on social media, and be sure to subscribe to Hala Taha's *Young and Profiting* podcast. The point is, these individuals are world changers, and if you implement the gold that they bring, you can change *your* world.

My promise to you is simple: if you consistently practice and apply the advice, suggestions, and life lessons from the heavy hitters featured in this book, your life and mindset will grow in direct proportion to the amount of action you take.

You will have better relationships, earn more money, and feel better about yourself. These things are happening with me and practically everyone featured in this book.

You might even grow to feel unstoppable.

Don't keep denying yourself access to a better life. Lord knows I've done that a million times more than anyone I've ever known. If you don't believe you deserve everything you want, you stand no chance of getting it. Having a better life requires "trying" no matter how much self-doubt you have.

I'm with you on this never-ending journey of self-fulfillment. Turn to the next page, and let's start growing together.

I got you.

Part I: Your Thinking Sucks. Let's Fix It.

You got an "F" on that test. You didn't make the football team. You didn't get accepted into Harvard law school.

Damn loser.

That's right. Whoever thinks you failed by not achieving those goals is the real loser. *You* are the winner because you didn't let the fear of failure, insecurities, or self-doubt stop you from trying.

As long as you learn from that bad grade or that exclusion from the team and tried again, you will never be a loser or "failure."

When we are children just starting school, most of us are taught that winning (or success) is good and losing (or failure) is bad. I kinda understand why we get programmed that way, but it sets us on the wrong path because that "wisdom" or advice is incomplete.

The foundation of success is rooted in trying and "failing," but society's perception and definition of failing seem to be "any effort that doesn't result in the desired outcome."

But I've come to view success as making an effort to try to do something legal and worthwhile (at least to the person doing it) while gritting your teeth through the inevitable challenges.

There also needs to be wisdom gained from whatever didn't go as planned and a refusal to give up on the pursuit of whatever you're attempting to achieve.

This section is designed to bring you new insights and perspectives on how to view winning and losing. You'll understand how flawed your thinking has become and how to fix it to set yourself up for victory.

Buckle up.

1.
NEWSFLASH: YOU'RE A COWARD

"He was just a coward and that was the worst luck any man could have."

—Ernest Hemingway

I'll be gentle when I say this. When it comes to trying something outside of your comfort zone, you're a bigger coward than the jurors who didn't have the guts to convict O.J.

That's your dirty truth, and guess what else? The biggest difference between you and Scooby-Doo facing a monster is that he can admit he's terrified.

Not you.

You just deny it and lie to yourself about your lack of self-belief. What if you try and fail? What if you get rejected? What if things just don't go your way?

Those terrifying questions run through your head faster than an ice-cream brain freeze, systematically destroying opportunities that you were too chicken shit to take.

How do I know?

Because I've long been the president of the world organization of cowards, and that B.S. fucks with my head like a disloyal girlfriend.

FLASHBACK: Sunday, September 25, 2011

As the clock inched past 3 am, I hurried down the steps of a college bar near Kent State University. Making my way through a chattering pack of young adults, I noticed they were either buzzed or blitzed from hours of drinking beers and shots.

I was in town with my crew to host my second public event to increase interest in my shocking web series, *a Date with Deantè*. Based on the flirtatious body and verbal language of a few young women, my guys and I were perceived as possessing some level of celebrity, and "beer goggles" certainly helped that perception.

It was impossible not to notice that several chicks were offering up their goodies like nonprofit vending machines! During the previous few hours, I had filmed several explicitly worded interviews with eager ladies for inclusion in my then-upcoming DVD.

Because of the reaction from the crowd and many other factors, this event qualified as a success, a sharp contrast to my first event held just five weeks earlier.

But when the time came to plan and schedule the next event, I made only a single phone call to a bar that I was considering for the venue. After that, I became a full-blown coward.

I never admitted it, but I subconsciously became overwhelmed at the idea of putting on another public event because I was afraid that it was going to suck.

Instead, I basked in my satisfying glory of the recently completed second event and allowed that to fulfill me. In other words, my self-belief secretly jumped off a cliff without a parachute.

That was a decade ago, and I continue to feel a sense of frustration at that version of myself. I spent an entire year "planning" how my events would function while convincing myself that I was making progress.

But I was just avoiding taking the next step. Secretly, I feared failure like R. Kelly fears having sex with adult women.

No one's going to shoot you if you screw up

It makes no sense to allow fear to stop you from trying things that feel intimidating. Think about the worst possible outcome if you "fail," and you'll see it's usually ridiculously unimportant.

If my third public event in 2011 had turned out to be a bigger flop than Vanilla Ice—so what? Nobody was going to shoot me for putting on a lousy event. There wasn't going to be a starving grizzly bear attacking me because my event sucked worse than Bill Cosby's release from prison, so what difference would it have made?

At worst, people would have made fun of me if I had put on a horrible event. I may have felt humiliated, and the whole nonsense would've lasted between 12 hours and eight days.

I could've dealt with that!

If I imagined some loose cannon shooting me like a deer in the country or arresting me over failing to meet the crowd's expectations (or my own), that would've been frightening!

None of that would've happened, so, therefore, I needlessly destroyed the hard-earned momentum I'd built for years.

And I still feel that I have unfinished business.

EVICT THE IDIOTS TAKING UP SPACE IN YOUR HEAD

Most of our fear comes from the expectations of others. We tend to let the opinions of others dictate our actions and even the way we feel about ourselves.

Ever since I attended elementary school, I have been a slave to the thoughts and standards of my peers. They could control me with their mockery or disapproval of my over-calinated physique, off-brand clothes, or nappy hair.

Laugh or judge all you want, but it's a guarantee that you've experienced the same crap on some level. I've learned that anyone taking up residence in my head needs to be issued a "cease to exist" letter.

Take your cues from a ticked-off landlord and evict those knuckleheads. No one should ever be allowed to take up space in your head with negative energy, so when you limit or second guess yourself, you're allowing them to control you.

Stop that!

It'll take practice but learn to operate from a place of power. This means possessing self-awareness of your inner strength and greatness and an inner belief that your feelings are what matters.

PREVENT THE EXCRUCIATING PAIN OF REGRET

The only thing worse than the pain of failure is the pain of regret, by far. Even though I was criticized consistently for producing such a controversial reality series, I never regretted doing it. I was called "fat nigger" more times than a calculator could count, and it energized me. Many took exception to how my guests were depicted in my episodes, even though the guests were consenting adults whose words and actions were their own.

I had tons of fans, but the haters and critics were unsettling at times. I largely ignored them, although I feared for my safety at several points because of threats made against me. Still, during that time and ever since then, I never held regrets for what I created. I do, however, regret that the show never had any closure because I didn't challenge myself to produce a final season or take it further than I did. But I am planning something very interesting in connection with that show in the near future.

Make it your business to prevent regretting "not doing" or "not trying" because it will rip you to shreds mentally. The only way to do that is to dive in when you feel resistance, but only with things you truly want to do.

Tell yourself that you're unstoppable by mankind, and only God and your fear can stop you.

Keep in Mind

- It makes no sense to allow fear to stop you from trying things that feel intimidating. Think about the worst possible outcome if you "fail," and you'll see it's usually ridiculously unimportant.

- Most of our fear comes from the expectations of others. We have a tendency to let the opinions of others dictate our actions and the way we feel about ourselves. Take your cues from a ticked-off landlord and evict those knuckleheads.

- Make it your business to prevent regretting "not doing" or "not trying" because it will rip you to shreds mentally.

2.
APPROPRIATE FEAR IS A GIFT

"Don't take anything lightly. Nothing comes easy. A little bit of fear is motivating. It doesn't mean you're scared. It means you're smart."

—Gregg Popovich

Renowned San Antonio Spurs coach Gregg Popovich coined the phrase "appropriate fear" years ago. It remains one of the best ways to describe the terror we sometimes feel—yet need to feel—when we step outside our comfort zone for a worthy cause. I know it sounds insane, but fear is actually a gift when used correctly, leveraging it to push you forward.

For example, I am terrified at the thought of building and running a multi-media company because of the sheer level of focus and resilience that it will require. My fear is bigger than seeing R. Kelly released from prison and headed to the nearest playground! But my fear of *not* making an effort to do it is much bigger because I believe that it's my destiny to fulfill. I won't survive the inevitable regret that I will have if I don't try with all my might.

THE HIGHEST FORM OF RESPECT

Getting a nervous feeling in your stomach like a thousand butterflies swirling around is a sure-fire sign that you're facing something that is a big deal. It is excitement disguised as nervous anticipation, which means your body and mind are giving that task or goal a shit ton of respect.

Actually, I'd say it's the highest form of respect because the resistance that you feel comes only with big things that matter to you. When the stakes are high, daring to try something can feel more frightening than a slumber party at Bill Cosby's house! Understand that anything worth doing is supposed to feel intimidating, so fighting against the body's natural tendency to avoid difficulty is perfectly normal.

In September 2020, I started a daily exercise regimen at the YMCA. To my utter amazement, I managed to be very consistent, even in the face of the occasional adversity and constant feeling of not wanting to put in the effort to go. By early February 2021, I had strung together 99 workouts in 21 weeks, and I felt great about myself.

Coincidentally, my 100th workout terrified me, like meeting Freddy Krueger in a never-ending dream. It was my first workout with Jonathan Church, a fitness coach, and he "took my soul," as David Goggins would say.

I hired two different fitness coaches; Jonathan and Julius Chisholm because I felt it was time for me to elevate the intensity level of my workouts. I had gotten very comfortable in my self-managed YMCA workouts, but I knew I had to evolve. My fear was a gift because I decided I didn't want to be pushed around by it.

I knew I wasn't ready mentally to take that bold step, but that's how we get better; by starting before we feel ready.

Your Premium Fuel

Think of yourself as a high-end sports car or luxury sedan. Those vehicles perform best when filled with premium fuel, and you will, too. Your premium fuel is your self-doubts and fear of trying things. I don't care if it's applying for a high-level job or speaking in public; let that fear fuel your mind to act in the face of your own doubts.

Recently, my cousin Torre asked me to speak at his wedding reception because he felt that I was best equipped to do it. More than one hundred people attended the event.

I have always been a "people person," but giving a meaningful speech to a crowd that size was a bit intimidating. I was nervous, but that fueled me to lock in and meet the moment with self-assurance. When I stepped to the microphone, I felt emotionally naked as all eyes in the room focused on me.

Then, I absolutely crushed it!

The strong reactions from the huge crowd allowed me to masterfully evoke every emotion that I wanted with my words: laughter, compassion, sentimentality, and awe. I felt like an unassailable force of nature because I achieved command of the room, and it all started because I allowed my nervousness and fear to fuel me.

That's exactly how you need to attack things that you want to do but are fearful of doing. Strive to achieve command of your effort and be unconcerned with the outcome.

The Mental Edge is Addicting

I committed to writing and publishing 100 articles during December 2020 to test my resilience and consistency. When I mentioned it to people, I received many shocked responses and a typical "that's crazy" from most. I expected it to be challenging, but once I was in the middle of it, I was even surprised at the daily dedication required to meet my goal. Going into the final day of December, I had successfully written and published 94 articles which was astounding to me. But I still needed to write and publish six more that final day, and I was massively mentally exhausted. I managed to hit my goal an hour and a half before the month was over.

That made me feel a thousand feet tall because I knew that most people would never even attempt something so challenging and all-encompassing, let alone stick with it to its conclusion. The book that you're reading right now is my third one this year, which is highly abnormal for most writers. My point is doing difficult things, even when they're intimidating, gives you an edge because most people don't do difficult things. The mental advantage you gain from using the gift of reasonable fear to push you forward then becomes addicting. You will also start feeling better about yourself, especially if you keep doing it!

Keep In Mind

- Getting a nervous feeling in your stomach like a thousand butterflies swirling around is a sure-fire sign that you're facing something that is a big deal. It is excitement disguised as nervous anticipation, which means your body and mind are giving that task or goal a shit ton of respect.

- Think of yourself as a high-end sports car or luxury sedan. Those vehicles perform best when filled with premium fuel, and you will, too. Your premium fuel is your self-doubts and fear of trying things. I don't care if it's applying for a high-level job or speaking in public; let that fear fuel your mind to take action.

- Doing difficult things, even when they're intimidating, gives you a huge edge because most people don't do difficult things.

3.
FOR THE RECORD, YOU'RE A SPOILED ASS BRAT

"Acknowledging the good that you already have in your life is the foundation for all abundance."

—Eckhart Tolle

As I lay conscious and confused in a hospital bed at Mercy Medical Center in September 2003, I had more nervous energy than Bill Clinton seeing that stained dress.

At my bedside were my twenty-one-year-old fiancé and my two-month-old daughter, Desireè. I was wracked with fear and disbelief, mainly because a nurse had come into the room asking me if I wanted to make out a Will. That was a horrifying thought, but the fact that nobody knew what in the hell was wrong with me was almost too much to handle.

I had been to the ER several times during the previous three months because I was experiencing a very jittery feeling in my chest that was unsettling at best. My heart rate almost always felt elevated, and I believed that I would collapse at any moment.

My many visits to the ER turned up nothing and caused more frustration. I assumed that whatever issue I had was related to being over-caloried, yet each physician who met with me dismissed that idea. Although shocking, that served as a little bit of relief. I experienced similar episodes seven years prior, and nothing conclusive ever came from that.

At Mercy Medical Center, I continued to fight off thoughts that I might not be around much longer to enjoy the two most important people in the world to me at the time, my lovely fiancé and beautiful baby girl.

I shared a room with an eighty-year-old man. At only twenty-six, the doctor told me that I was the youngest person ever admitted to the "cardiology floor," which was awesome and awful at the same time. With so many terrible thoughts in my mind, I realized how much I didn't want to die and lose the great things in my life.

The jitteriness in my chest didn't go away for several more months, but the huge benefit of those moments of uncertainty is the considerable mindset shift I achieved.

My previous complaints seemed trivial and pathetic at that point. I began realizing and voicing how enormously lucky and blessed I was, and nearly two decades later, that belief has only gotten stronger.

How would you view your "problems" or "issues" if you felt that you might die any second? I can only speculate on what your answer might be, but I do know one thing for certain:

You're a spoiled ass brat.

Trust Me, You're the Luckiest Person in the World

Being you is the ultimate privilege, but you act like you don't know that shit. Instead, you tend to think about everyone else's "advantages," which is a pathetic mindset to have. As long as your thinking is off, you won't be capable of understanding the tremendous upside to trying and failing. That will make you less likely to step outside of your comfort zone and try things despite feeling you may fail.

Start telling yourself that you are the luckiest person in the world because your gifts, talents, experiences, and perspective were only given to *you*. You would never be willing to trade the great people in your life, whether your children, co-workers, friends, or family, for anyone. They are irreplaceable, and you need to grasp that concept because it makes the pain of "failure" or "rejection" so much easier to digest. Imagine applying for a high-paying career at a prestigious company but not getting hired. It would suck and might even feel devastating, but you'd still have all of your priceless experiences and the fabulous people in your life. You didn't lose the most important things in your life, which means that you are the luckiest person in the world—your world.

Taking Your Blessings for Granted is a Huge Risk

During those terrifying months in 2003, I felt that I could be gone any second. The nervous feeling in my chest and what seemed to be an always racing heart humbled me in many ways. I became more aware of the blessings in my life, and it was awful to imagine having all that goodness taken from me. My mindset became more focused on being grateful for every minor or major thing I had going for me.

If you are anything like I was, you need to stop taking your blessings for granted because they can quickly be taken away. Train yourself to think positive thoughts because negative thoughts manifest negative outcomes, and positive thoughts manifest positive outcomes. Each day when I show up at the gym, one of the women at the front desk asks me, "How's your day?"

Like clockwork, my response is unique and decisive; "My day is absolutely spectacular" or "My day is extraordinary." There are multiple benefits to this: It sends a message to my subconscious that I have positive thoughts and I convey positive emotion to others. It also tends to infuse the person on the receiving end of that message with a pleasant thought, even if it's brief. I'm not lying when I say that my day is spectacular. I'm simply conveying what the awareness of my blessings causes me to think.

Within the first few minutes of waking, God blessed me with another day of breathing, seeing, thinking, the ability to stand and walk on my own feet (not artificial), a roof over my head, peace, serenity, and endless opportunities. He blessed you with some or all of those things, or even more, which makes me think, "How can this be a bad day when I have been given all of those blessings?" My advice to you: think the same way.

Get Over Your Sense of Entitlement

You're a spoiled brat because you already have so much, yet you're so ungrateful for that. You want more things or better things which is absolutely okay. But it's not okay to give a mental middle finger to what you currently have just because you want other things. Be grateful, or you will regret it one day. I have a friend with malformed legs who has been in a wheelchair practically since birth. I have another friend who lost his mom and his long-term marriage during the same timeframe. I know several people who were either raped, given up for adoption, lived in foster homes, suffer from depression and anxiety, have been in prison, and/or been destroyed by drug abuse. I am supremely grateful that none of those things have been my reality to this point, so my life is great, and your life is also great.

True, I don't know your situation, but even if you suffer from any of situations that I just mentioned, there are always things that you have going for you that are wonderful. Ask yourself: "What awesome person or thing in my life makes my life better than it would be if they were taken from my life?" I saw this posted on Facebook earlier today:

> *"Be happy with what you have while you are working for what you want. Be humble and patient."*

Get over your self-entitlement.

Keep in Mind:

- Being you is the ultimate privilege, but you act like you don't know that shit. Instead, you tend to think about everyone else and their "advantages," which is a pathetic mindset to have.

- Stop taking your blessings for granted because they can quickly be taken from you. Train yourself to have positive thoughts because negative thoughts manifest negative outcomes, and positive thoughts manifest positive outcomes.

- You want more things, or better things which is absolutely okay. But it's not okay to give a mental middle finger to what you currently have just because you want other things. Be grateful, or you will regret it one day.

4.
IF YOU KNEW YOU WERE GONNA FAIL, WHAT WOULD YOU DO?

"I can accept failure; everyone fails at something. But I can't accept not trying."

—Michael Jordan

Best-selling author and thought leader Seth Godin offered a fascinating new take on the age-old question, "If you knew you wouldn't fail, what would you do?" He views that question as absolutely worthless and instead offers a far more useful one: "If you knew you were gonna fail, what would you do?" Asking yourself that question will illuminate what truly matters the most to you because, let's face it, unless we're suicidal, none of us would walk or drive across a train track if we knew we would fail. We would only cross it because we believe we will succeed and come out unharmed, so there's minimal risk (unless the red lights are flashing and the bars are down).

Knowing that we *will* fail at something and choosing to do it anyway speaks volumes about what fulfills us or what is most urgent in our lives. In my opinion, it is one of the best barometers of self-awareness that there is.

26 · IF YOU KNEW YOU WERE GONNA FAIL, WHAT WOULD YOU DO?

How Deep is Your Love?

If you knew you would fail at getting your desired outcome, what occupation would you pursue? What person or relationship would you chase? One moment sticks out in my mind. I foolishly risked my safety to pursue something because my love was so strong. In 2010, my popularity and reputation in my neighborhood and surrounding communities grew quickly because of my online reality series, *a Date with Deantè*. As I neared the end of production of Season Three, I conducted a filmed interview with a young woman who was a friend of my then "girlfriend."

My show was highly controversial, and my line of questioning was very Howard Sternesque, so many people took offense to how my guests were depicted. I was often branded an exploiter of women, especially since the series was comedy-based. When the episode featuring this woman was released online, many of her friends got more pissed than the underpants of a passed-out alcoholic. A local bar owner and a few regulars were so angry at "how bad" I "made her look" in the episode that they got downright racist in their contempt for me.

"If that nigger ever tries to step foot in this bar, he won't make it past the front door," the owner supposedly said about me. Most of the regulars supported that thinking, and when my "girlfriend" told me about that, I was heavily offended. Not because of their white supremacist language, but because I felt they underestimated me in thinking I would accept that I couldn't walk into that bar. My passion was strong for the movement and momentum I had created with nearly seventy episodes of *a Date with Deantè* over an almost four-year period. I believed my job was to not only push the envelope with its content but bulldoze it into a million pieces.

I told my "girlfriend" (a white woman) that I was going to walk into that bar and interview on camera a few of the racist regulars to feature in a future episode of my series. I also predicted that the racist owner would give me a free drink before I left. My girl and another of her (white) female friends drove us to the bar. Although I was nervous and a bit scared on the inside, I walked confidently through the door with my camera and model release forms. There were about two dozen patrons in the place, all white folks. It definitely looked like a Klan rally up in that bitch.

I heard someone say "nigger" a few moments after I walked in, which was a bit unsettling since I was standing there with the two white women surrounded by a bar full of tipsy Caucasian racists. I talked a bit of smack to the owner and challenged him to go on camera and spout off his racist views. He agreed, and a few customers followed suit. Everyone signed release forms and stepped outside in the rear of the bar to begin filming.

The film shoot lasted around forty-five minutes, and it was intimidating and pathetic. My adrenaline and passion for creating thought-provoking content that would shock and entertain my viewers dwarfed my nervous energy. I was a bit worried that I wouldn't make it out of this hole-in-the-wall pit of vile discrimination unharmed, but I made it out just fine. I also convinced the owner to give me and my girl free Crown Royal drinks (that I watched him make). In the days and weeks that followed, a lot of evil and awfulness came upon me as a result of that Sunday afternoon "activity." At a certain point, I feared for my safety and life and was advised by loved ones not to go anywhere in public alone.

28 · IF YOU KNEW YOU WERE GONNA FAIL, WHAT WOULD YOU DO?

My actions were dangerous and shortsighted and could have easily ended in tragedy. But my passion for my artistic endeavors (my show) was at or near its apex, rendering the possibility or likelihood of failure irrelevant. My simple question for you: is there anything in this life that you love as deeply as I did creating my series? I encourage you to do some serious soul searching to discover the answer because I know there's something you love at that level, so go all-in on whatever that is.

Adopt the Gambler's Mindset

Always remember this: you are your number one investment, and I advise you to go all-in on that investment. I am not here to portray myself as a guy who has an unchallenged belief in myself because I don't. I also fall short time and time again on trying and doing in the face of fear and uncertainty, but I have improved my self-belief and willingness to take action on a massive scale, and I want to help you do the same. One way to help your fear of failure is to adopt the gambler's mindset.

When I was a kid, my grandmother was obsessed with playing the lottery. She often had very little money to pay for all of her needs, but she was fearless about gambling away chunks of cash. Like every other gambler, the slim odds of winning were worth it to her despite the overwhelming odds of losing. Grandma would lose probably 99% of the times she played, and when she won, it was mostly tiny amounts as small as $41.50. I've seen this phenomenon with scratch-off tickets and in casinos, but the huge super lotto or Mega Millions jackpot really gets people to take action in the face of astronomical odds against them.

According to a recent report on CNBC, a Mega Millions lottery drawing had reached $970 million, and the odds of winning that jackpot was one in 302.5 million! Most shocking to me is the much better odds of becoming a billionaire, which according to titlemax.com, is one in 578,508! Granted, it will take many years to amass that kind of wealth if it's not handed down to you, whereas the lottery jackpot would be instant. But still.

If we took the same fearless approach to achieving important yet uncomfortable things in life, the possibilities would be truly endless!

THE FAMOUS MICHAEL JORDAN COMMERCIAL

In 1997, the brilliant minds at Nike released a television ad to promote the latest Air Jordan sneaker. Michael Jordan starred in the thirty-second ad, but the golden asset of the commercial were these words, delivered in a voiceover by MJ:

> *"I've missed more than 9,000 shots in my career. I've lost almost 300 games. 26 times I've been trusted to take the game-winning shot and missed. I've failed over, and over, and over again in my life. And that is why—I succeed."*

This quote has become an iconic emblem of the relationship between perseverance and success in the nearly quarter-century since the ad first hit the airwaves,. Placing a legendary, highly accomplished figure like Jordan in the ad and highlighting his actual "failures" was a stroke of pure genius. The message is loud and resounding: You win because of your many failings, and the more you "fail," the more you will succeed. Take that mindset and run with it, and I'll be right there with you because we all need that lesson!

Keep in Mind

- If you knew you would fail at getting your desired outcome, what occupation would you pursue? What person or relationship would you chase? I encourage you to do some serious soul searching to discover the answer, because I know you love something at that level, so go all-in on whatever that is.

- You are your number one investment, and I advise you to go all in on that investment. Adopt the gambler's mindset to help your fear of failure.

- You win because of your many failings, and the more you "fail," the more you will succeed. Take that mindset and run with it, and I'll be right there with you because we all need that lesson!

5.
THE 90% RULE:
MY POSITIVE ENERGY FORMULA

*"Keep your face to the sunshine
and you cannot see the shadow."*

—Helen Keller

As I sat frustrated in the SUV that I had rented for the week, I sighed and rolled my eyes what felt like a million times. That's the kind of thing I do when I've been waiting fifteen minutes for something that should've taken less than three.

My birthday was the following day, and it's become a tradition for me to spend time with people that are practically a lock to make my day better in some way with very minimal chance of negativity. I try to do that every day, but I'm more intentional about that when it's my birthday and the immediate days before and after.

The SUV was located in the parking lot of a corner store. My cousin went inside to get a few items that should've resulted in a quick in and out. When he finally came out of the store, my patience was near a breaking point. I soon reminded myself that I willingly signed up for a situation I knew ahead of time would fall far outside of *The 90% Rule*, so it was nobody's fault but my own.

The 90% Rule is my positive energy formula. In a nutshell, I consider past experiences and current social reputations of people to determine if I'm going to invest time in their presence. If there's a less than 90% chance that I'll enjoy time spent with them with zero regrets about the experience, I give little to no time to that person. If the estimate is 90% or above, I feel that it's a virtual guarantee that I'll love the time spent.

This particular cousin has a long-standing reputation for bringing a drama-filled bullshit vibe with him anywhere he goes. But I love reminiscing with him about our shared childhood and young adult moments from decades ago, which is why I bit the bullet to chill with him.

If you want to be a winner, have a happier life, or both, I recommend that you adopt *The 90% Rule* because positive surroundings and influences are mandatory for that lifestyle.

Pick Your Vibe, Be That Vibe, Then Find Your Tribe

I'm assuming that you want to be happier and more successful, so you'll need to manifest that. You can't be hanging around shameless crackheads when you want a kick-ass lifestyle. Don't get it twisted; you don't have to be rich to have a magnificent life...it's more about your mindset and having the valuable components of your life in place.

So, if your vibe is to be happier and more successful, you need to do things that invite those realities into your life. I write personal development books because they help others, but they also help me the most. As an author and owner of a fledgling multimedia company, I am constantly gaining leverage in the marketplace and social circles, one teeny tiny step at a time.

I have hired personal growth and fitness coaches and surround myself with people who are further along than I am on the journey to financial and entrepreneurial abundance. You need to take similar steps if you want that type of life. I picked my vibe, and I am intentionally becoming that vibe. Finding my tribe goes hand in hand with all that because I put myself in situations where they are already showing up.

Don't Be Misery's Company

I've been around many people who are just not happy with their lives. They complain about their circumstances, talk shit about other people who are doing better than them, and usually hang around people who do the same.

Steer clear of those muthafuckas!

I would become so frustrated in the presence of people like that. I wondered why they couldn't just be grateful for the good in their lives. Eventually, I did a bit of soul searching and realized I needed to let negative pessimists hang out among themselves.

That's also my advice to you: *Don't complain about the negative energy of others; make it your responsibility to find environments congruent with your life's vision.* There's a reason you won't find a polar bear in Punta Cana or an alligator in Alaska.

Keep Developing Yourself

If you're deliberately seeking out positive energy people to hang around, it's necessary to also work on the value and positive energy you bring to the world. I read and study books and articles, search for lessons in every experience and lead with kindness. I am not perfect with any of this, and I don't need to be. My default setting is humor and friendliness, but I'm also human and fall short at times. Don't beat yourself up when the same happens to you; learn from it and try to show up better the next time.

Listen to those who point out some of your less-than-stellar qualities. What annoying or negative habits or energy do you notice about yourself? Fix it to become a more significant asset and resource for others, and you'll be amazed at how positively that will affect you and your life.

Keep in Mind

- You can't be hanging around shameless crackheads when you want a kick-ass lifestyle.

- Let negative pessimists hang among themselves. Don't complain about others' negative energy; make it your responsibility to find environments congruent with the vision for your life.

- If you're deliberately seeking out positive energy people to hang around, it's necessary to also work on the value and positive energy you bring to the world.

Part II: Legendary Tales of The Illusion of Failure

Steph Curry *missed* 484 three-pointers in his incredibly amazing MVP season of 2015-16. That means the superstar guard of the Golden State Warriors averaged slightly above six *MISSED* threes per game that season. He is almost universally regarded as the greatest three-point shooter in NBA history and has heavily influenced the way modern basketball is played at all levels.

Yet, this extraordinary basketball marksman, during one of the most phenomenal offensive seasons in league history, managed to miss nearly 500 of the shot of which he is most proficient.

Knowing only those numbers makes Steph seem like a huge failure when it comes to shooting a basketball. But to those of us who know hoops, Curry is such a brilliant offensive juggernaut that he often seems professorial in his detailed approach to shooting with extreme accuracy from deep.

That 2015-16 season was a watershed time for Steph as he achieved the incredibly rare 50/40/90 split. That's at least 50% (50.4) shooting on all field goals, 40% (45.4) on threes, and 90% (90.8) on foul shots. This feat had only been accomplished ten times by seven different players in the entire seven-decade history of the NBA (three more since counting Steph's).

In other words, Curry's 484 missed threes were simply the *illusion* of failure. Making an attempt and not giving up when things don't go your way is what matters most in life.

As a result, he became the first-ever player to connect on an astonishing 400 threes (402) in a single season. In this chapter, I detail three other famous examples of the illusion of failure that led to massive success worldwide.

Be inspired.

6.
Michael Jordan Will Never Win a Championship

June 14, 1998: "Tired as Hell"

A career defined by excellence, world-class achievement, and stubborn competitiveness came down to possibly the greatest challenge of Michael Jordan's legendary run in the NBA.

With his Chicago Bulls gunning for a sixth league championship in eight seasons, MJ found himself stuck in a shooting slump at the worst possible time: mid-fourth quarter in Game 6 of the 1998 NBA finals. With age, limited offense from his teammates, and a revenge-seeking Utah Jazz team to battle, Jordan kept missing critical jump shots—five in a row, to be exact.

I was on pins and needles watching on television almost 1,800 miles away from the site of this terrifyingly close game. I kept telling myself that Michael would somehow find a way to will his team to victory, which would result in the Bulls' second three-peat of the decade. If they lost (God forbid), they would face a do-or-die Game 7 against a most certainly more raucous Utah team and crowd once again on the road.

Both astonishing and expected, Jordan summoned his signature killer instinct and managed to score Chicago's final eight points of the game. But his three legacy inflating plays happened after the Jazz went up 86-83 with just 41.9 seconds remaining in the game.

MJ scored on a driving layup, stole the ball from Utah superstar Karl Malone, then nailed a "go fuck yourself" jumper with 5.2 seconds left that served as the winning basket. Timeout, Jazz.

Thirty-five and running on fumes, Jordan would later say that he was "tired as hell" as he sat on the bench during Utah's timeout. Moments later, Michael Jordan had captured the sixth NBA finals MVP of his historic career as he led the Bulls to their sixth championship since 1991.

As impressive as MJ's trying and failing over and over was in the fourth quarter of that final game, it pales in comparison to what it took to reach that lofty position in sports history. He and the Bulls stood tall in June 1998 with six championship trophies. But in June 1990, Michael had completed six NBA seasons with zero championships on his resume. By that point, his individual greatness was unquestioned and unimpeachable. But there was one phrase that the media and some fans began to say more often than not:

Michael Jordan will never win a championship.

1984-1987: "God Disguised as Michael Jordan"

Michael Jordan had a decorated career as a collegiate player at the University of North Carolina and a spectacular showing at the 1984 summer Olympics. Still, no one was prepared for his explosive rise to superstardom in the NBA. Aided by an almost unreasonably large chip on his shoulder and physics-defying athleticism, MJ ripped through his first NBA season like a blowtorch through ice cream. Before MJ joined the Chicago Bulls, the team had only made the playoffs once in the previous seven seasons and had won just 33% of their games in 1983-84.

The good news: The Bulls qualified for the NBA playoffs in each of MJ's first three seasons. *The bad news*: Each of those years ended with lightning-quick exits in the first round of the postseason. During his inaugural campaign of 1984-85, Jordan proved himself to be a tireless worker in practice, which paid off with his selection to the All-Rookie First Team thanks to his extraordinary production (28.2 points, 6.5 rebounds, 5.9 assists). Predictably, he was named the *Rookie of the Year* while establishing himself as a bona fide megastar in a league of superstars.

None of that mattered when facing the Milwaukee Bucks in the first round of the playoffs. After the dust settled, the Bulls lost that series 1-3 and began looking towards the following season.

MJ's second season, 1985-86, was immediately marred when the high-flying guard suffered a stress fracture to his foot in the third game of the season. Mike missed 64 games but returned to ignite a late-season playoff push allowing the Bulls to enter the playoffs as the lowest seed. That earned them the right to match up with the dominant Boston Celtics, who towered over the NBA with a 67-15 record, including an eye-popping 40-1 mark on their home court.

In what has become one of the most iconic NBA playoff games in history, Jordan set a still-standing record by scoring 63 points in Game 2. His dynamic energy and endless appetite for competition were on full display, though he failed to lead his team to victory in both that game and the series. Chicago got punched in the mouth again in the playoffs, this time in a clean 0-3 sweep at the hands of Larry Legend and the rest of the eventual champion Celtics.

MJ returned for the 1986-87 season with a completely healed foot and a new head coach. The Bulls brought in Doug Collins, who understood Michael's stunning excellence on the court and promptly kept the ball in his hands as much as possible. By the end of Jordan's third season, he led the NBA in scoring at a scorching 37.1 points per game. He became the first player in nearly a quarter-century to amass 3,000 points in a single season, yet the very talent-starved Bulls held a losing record of 40-42 heading into the playoffs.

Once again, the defending champion Celtics stood tall against Chicago and kicked them in the teeth while serving up another 3-0 sweep. Three seasons in, and Michael Jordan had proven that individual brilliance is wonderful to look at but won't get you very far by itself. Sure, his teammates were the general equivalent of a box of squashed raisins, but as the team's pre-eminent force, MJ needed to grow as a leader and gain more qualified players around him.

1987-1990: Come Fly with Me

The 1987 draft was particularly fruitful for the Bulls. GM Jerry Krause used deft maneuvering to acquire small forward Scottie Pippen in a draft-day trade with the Seattle Supersonics. Chicago also drafted Horace Grant to take over the power forward role occupied by Charles Oakley.

Though neither player was expected to be a star in their first year, they were promising young talents who could blossom into key players in the near future.

Michael Jordan continued his high-scoring, high-flying attack on the league during the 1987-88 season. He elevated his game defensively and dominated awards season while leading the NBA in scoring for the second consecutive year (35.0 points per game).

MJ also earned his first league MVP award, led the NBA in steals and minutes played, and was named Defensive Player of the Year. Though rookies Pippen and Grant contributed minimal production statistically, it was clear that there was significant potential in them, and they helped the Bulls post their first 50-win season of the Jordan Era.

Scottie, in particular, was pivotal in the opening round of the NBA playoffs vs. the Cleveland Cavaliers as he and Michael led the Bulls to their first playoff series win, 3-2.

Unfortunately for Chicago, the Detroit Pistons were their next matchup in the semifinals round. They were a far more talented team top to bottom than the Bulls, and they had Jordan in their crosshairs.

After MJ torched the Pistons with a 59-point scoring performance during the regular season, the "Bad Boys" (as they were known) implemented a brutal and overly physical defensive scheme to trap MJ with double teams and rough house tactics.

The Bulls lost that series 1-4.

The 1988-89 season produced an even more dominant Pistons team. After beating Chicago, they beat the Celtics to meet the Lakers in the finals and lost in seven games. That explains their elevated level of focus in 1988-89 as they raced to a 63-19 record while the Bulls seemed to take a step back, winning just 47 games.

The addition of veteran center Bill Cartwright added more experience and versatility at center while Pippen and Grant added to their games and became more critical to the team's success.

Michael was still Michael. He led the league for the third consecutive season in scoring (32.5 points per game) and elevated his status as the game's most exciting player. Chicago once again met their division rivals, the Cavaliers, in Round One of the playoffs.

The Cavs, however, beat the Bulls in all six regular season meetings head-to-head. They also boasted a very talented roster of players and were favored to beat Chicago in the series.

After four games, the series was tied at 2-2, with the deciding fifth game played in the Cavs' home arena. Jordan broke the hearts of many Ohioans when he capped a 44-point scoring burst with a buzzer-beating jump shot. That legendary shot fueled an improbable march through the postseason, yet the team hit the same brick wall as the previous postseason: the Pistons.

Bulls eliminated again, 2-4.

MJ opened his sixth pro season in an angry mood. He tortured the Cavs with a 54-point masterpiece as he and the Bulls entered a new phase of their journey. Phil Jackson came in as head coach and implemented the triangle offense to make it more difficult for other teams to defend Chicago, because the other players then had more chances to generate offense.

Despite the decreased shooting opportunities for Jordan, he still earned his fourth consecutive scoring title (33.6 points per game) while also netting a single-game career-high 69 points in a March game against Cleveland.

The Bulls looked sharper and better prepared to battle Detroit in the playoffs. Pippen was now an All-Star and Grant was solid on the boards. This combination added up to their best record yet, 55-27, entering the playoffs.

Jordan was predictably spectacular during the first two rounds as he averaged nearly 40 points per game. The Bulls held a 7-2 record heading into their second straight Eastern Conference finals series against the Pistons.

Chicago lost another physically demanding series to Detroit, this time 3-4. At this point, the sports media were loudly proclaiming Michael Jordan to be "the Ernie Banks of basketball," a super gifted individual incapable of leading a team to a championship.

Jordan was particularly emotional in the hours following the horrific blowout loss. He knew he needed to become better, stronger, and trust his teammates more. Losing for so many years led him to hire a trainer to bulk up.

Losing so much also led to him winning like crazy over the next eight years. That crushing defeat in June 1990 to the Pistons was the third consecutive series loss to that team. It was the sixth consecutive postseason that MJ tasted "failure."

All that shit did was create a goddamn monster. Six NBA championships later, and it makes sense that Jordan was "tired as hell" at the end of it all.

7.
Eminem Will Never Make it as a Rapper

When I first saw an utterly hilarious music video starring a skinny blonde-haired white guy on MTV in 1999, I was eager to find out who in the hell this person was.

He was full of witty rhymes, which felt more like incredibly clever punchlines, and before long, I found out who this lyrically brilliant hip-hop artist was.

Eminem.

During those early months of 1999, his popularity as the newest member of super-producer Dr. Dre's Aftermath record label seemed to have been launched from a cannon. Little did anyone know, but by the end of the following decade, his massive achievements and popularity in the music industry would earn him the coveted title of "Artist of the Decade" by Billboard magazine.

But nothing came easy in his formative years, and global fame was the least likely outcome for him. Except for one thing: Eminem never stopped trying to make his dream a reality.

The Race Challenge

In a country overwhelmingly dominated by the Caucasian race, Eminem found himself facing an unusual challenge. Trying to earn credibility in hip-hop throughout the 1990s as a white boy was a huge burden. The world of rap music had always been dominated by black artists and, with very few exceptions, white rappers were seen as a complete joke.

Vanilla Ice made matters worse when he showed up in the rap game in 1990. Despite massive success with "Ice, Ice Baby," his momentary fame soon dissolved, and he became a laughingstock. He was widely viewed as a talentless wannabe and a corny one-hit wonder.

This perception of white rappers essentially became universal in the industry and affected any "vanilla complected" artist who grabbed a microphone.

The Beastie Boys were comprised of three white-skinned guys, but their enormous success and influence felt different because they were a group.

Caucasian solo artists who tried to gain relevance in the industry had to deal with "reverse racism" because the most iconic artists were black, and white equaled "mediocre."

Eminem faced that discrimination every time he entered a rap competition, which was depicted in his 2002 film debut, *8 Mile*.

THE DARKEST HOUR IS JUST BEFORE DAWN

My grandmother used to say, "The darkest hour is just before dawn," meaning circumstances would get really bad just before getting really good, which was definitely the case for Eminem. As the 90s entered its final four years, the aspiring rapper lived a poverty-stricken existence in a crime-ridden neighborhood.

By the end of 1995, Eminem had a newborn daughter and a dysfunctional relationship with her mother, along with an equally dysfunctional relationship with his own mom. He continued to struggle for acceptance in local rap competitions, and his income was lousy.

His 1996 album, *Infinite* was heavily criticized while his drug use increased. A trip to Los Angeles in 1997 led Eminem down the path towards his breakthrough. He placed second in the rap Olympics but was impressive enough in his performance that his low-budget *The Slim Shady EP* landed in the hands of Interscope Records CEO Jimmy Iovine.

After listening to the EP, Dr. Dre immediately wanted to speak with Eminem.

LOSING BECOMES WINNING

Eminem appeared in *The Source* magazine in March 1998 in their popular "Unsigned Hype" section. Eleven months later, his major label debut album, *The Slim Shady LP* took the industry by storm, selling nearly 300,000 copies its first week. It took less than seven weeks to go platinum, with sales eclipsing one million, and in what felt like a flash of time to us, Eminem was a massive celebrity.

For the bleached blonde artist, it was a long and tough climb filled with many failures and setbacks. His remarkable talent was undeniable, but it was his refusal to give up on his vision that made his massive success possible.

Now 22 years after his first album, Eminem has long since crafted an enormous legacy in the world of hip-hop. He is among the foremost iconic artists in the game and earned a boatload of accolades for his excellence on the mic.

I am most impressed with his will to succeed in the face of extreme opposition to his race, lyrical content, and controversial subject matter.

Eminem proved his doubters wrong.

8.
Oprah Winfrey Will Never Make It in Television

Oprah Winfrey left an indelible mark on the world of television in 2011 when she ended her historic 25-year run as host of *The Oprah Winfrey Show*. That same year, she launched OWN, a television network aimed at lifestyle, wellness, and entertainment.

The history of television cannot be told without a significant profile of Oprah, but once upon a time, any success from her seemed nearly unthinkable.

Early Years Filled with Constant Trauma

Born into poverty, Oprah was also molested by relatives throughout her childhood and teens and impregnated at 14. Her baby died soon after birth which greatly affected her young mind.

Despite a few positive accomplishments (a radio job while in high school and winning a local beauty pageant), Oprah's life was a shit show.

Trying to Survive in a Man's World

Oprah had long held an interest in media and journalism. She studied communication in college and eventually landed a job as a news anchor in Nashville. Before long, she was co-anchoring the news in Baltimore but was soon demoted to a lower position.

By 1983, Oprah had moved on to Chicago, where she found success hosting *AM Chicago*. Perhaps a foreshadowing of things to come, Oprah took that show from last place to first, beating the long-tenured Phil Donahue in the ratings.

Relentlessness Pays Off

The Oprah Winfrey Show officially launched in September 1986 and would soon catapult its upstart namesake into the realm of highly scrutinized celebrity. The show rode a wave of momentum powered by Oprah's signature empathetic interview style and skyrocketed up the charts.

By the end of the 1980s, she had shockingly become the richest African American of the 20th century and, in 2003, the world's first black female billionaire.

I continue to marvel at how far perseverance and simply *trying* have carried Oprah Winfrey. She has been massively influential for decades and has lived a life of record-setting philanthropy and high-level achievement.

There's no question that "losing" so often built her into a winner!

Part III: How to Win 100% of the Time

In early 2011, actor Charlie Sheen went on a media blitz in which he spouted off what seemed to be a series of drug-induced nonsensical ramblings. It started on radio and continued in several television interviews leading to him coining the phrase, "Winning."

He used that single word to describe what he felt was the net result of a lifestyle that included vandalizing hotel rooms, endless sex with porn stars and prostitutes and consuming enormous amounts of drugs and alcohol.

It was seen in the media as a massive meltdown by a once-beloved Hollywood star, but I believe that Sheen really was "winning" at that moment. That's because his definition of the word was different from the official meaning.

If you want to win in life 100% of the time, you must do what Charlie Sheen did a decade ago: redefine what "winning" and "losing" is.

In the following section, the amazing journeys and mindsets of eighteen kick-ass individuals will blow your mind. Some are extremely wealthy; others are transformative figures in fitness and business, and all of them share a few common threads.

They have unique perspectives of what constitutes success and failure. They have the guts to point the finger at themselves when things don't go their way. They are champions not because of trophies, medals or currency, but because they all made the decision to never quit.

Get under their influence.

Note: The following interviews have been edited for time, grammar and clarity.

9.
SIMON ARIAS: THERE'S NO SUCCESS WITHOUT ADVERSITY

State Director and Owner of Arias Agencies/16 years in business

Simon Arias once told me that he wants the best of everything; the best woman, cars, and homes. But his astounding drive and commitment to excellence always feels like "the best of everything" anytime I speak with him or see him in motion. He is a truly gifted speaker, but if ever there was someone who walks the walk, it's this man. It is my privilege to present to you, Simon Anthony Arias, III.

—D.Y.

Deantè: *Based on your life experiences, how important has failure been to your success?*

Simon: I've learned there's no way to succeed without failure and by listening to others, being coachable, finding the right mentors, you can decrease the amount of failure you need to have to a very small amount. But you still must have failure, and there's no way to protect yourself 100% from having some struggles to grow something. I think it's been important in the sense that I discovered how to have a different relationship with failure because now I understand that it is a steppingstone to greatness.

Deantè: *Was there a specific event that caused you to understand it that way? When we're younger, we sometimes have difficulty understanding some of those things.*

Simon: Mostly in business, life, and relationships. My wife is not the only woman I've been with in the world, and I'm not the only man she's been with in the world, so that means I've failed at other relationships. I learned some of that could be avoidable if you're coachable and have the right mentors, but you gotta learn a lot of that stuff from experience and growth. You're young, you make mistakes and certain decisions, and the same thing applies in business. I can think of many things that I've failed at, but I can't pinpoint a time where "this one thing happened," causing me to have a different relationship with failure. It was more of a gradual thing of understanding my failed experiences and coming back from those realizing that I probably would've never achieved success if I had quit.

I think the problem is people fail because of their relationship with failure, believing "failure" has a period at the end instead of a comma. So, they stop trying instead of understanding that it's a part of that process. I've learned that you learn and grow from those failures by not quitting and watching what happens on the other side.

I also read books and study other great people I admire and have allowed the opportunity to influence my mind... people who've started large companies such as Nike. I read the book *Shoe Dog* by Phil Knight and realized how long this man had to fail and how many times this man had to fail. When I read the stories of Walt Disney, Sam Walton, and Phil Knight, the people that you look up to who are worth billions of dollars and help tons of people, I realized there's failure all throughout that sucker.

Most people would've quit during those failures. I'm reading about some of those stories and I'm like, "Whoa! How did that dude come back from that?" I realized that it wasn't just me—

anybody who wants to be anything and reach those levels will fail on their way to success.

Deantè: *Winning usually requires a lot of trial and error. On your journey so far, what were some of the biggest challenges to get you to where you are currently?*

Simon: My biggest challenge was myself. The hardest person to lead is the army of one. When you learn to conquer *yourself*, you then have an opportunity to possibly lead and help others conquer things. First, for me, it was my competitive nature. I wanted to win, and I wanted to win fast. Because I was young and immature when I first started the business, it was never good enough. I wasn't number one every week, every month in everything. I started to let it beat me up to the point where it became toxic to me instead of helping me, where usually that competitive nature allows me to drive and outwork people.

I was sabotaging myself because I lacked patience and wasn't thinking long-term about 'a year from today' or 'two years from today.' Instead of having an "if you're first, you're last" mentality, I learned to take a longer-term approach to things and that greatness requires a process. If you try to short-cut that process and "shoot steroids" into that process too much, you can hurt yourself accidentally. So, I started to beat myself when I was beating most people…I was already winning, but it wasn't enough. I had to get over it and understand that I can't force my beliefs on others.

I got to a point in my career where I knew what developing myself mentally, physically, and spiritually would do for my life. I put time into strengthening my relationship spiritually with the Lord. I committed to consistently exercising instead of making excuses that I didn't have time and reading books, although I hated to read and never read a book until I got out of college. I realized how much that did for my overall life as a human being because it helped me become a better son, father, person, and mentor and helped me get through struggles that I never would've gotten through. I want that for others, so I try to give them that. If they didn't follow the recipe, I would become so frustrated, causing people to run away from my business because I wanted them to be just like me in a sense.

I still want people to do that because I know what it will do for their life, but I've learned to have more patience and grace with others to allow them to make their own decisions. I can be here to guide, mentor, and provide the recipe, but like they say, "You can lead a horse to water but you can't make him drink," I don't run the horses off if they don't want to drink the exact water. Some of them will drink it in six months; others will drink it in twelve months. So, I had to learn patience in allowing people to be unique to themselves. If they want to follow the recipe, I know where it will get them, but now I give them the room to make their own choices.

Also, there are a lot of challenges to processing hate and having haters. There's only a certain level you can get to without having people who are upset because of your success. For some reason, they think your success makes them less of an individual. To this day, I don't think I'm better than anybody else. I'm blessed that I stood in welfare lines with my mother and grew up in a house that we sold for $11,000. So, I know where I come from, and I know the people there, and I love them and don't judge them.

I've been on a different end of the track, and there's good and bad in everything. I don't feel like I'm better than anybody because I have a successful business or I have a couple dollars in my pocket. If anything, I feel like I owe more to this world and other people to show them the way and share the resources. But even with that logic and mindset, I'm not perfect. The first thing a mentor will tell you is, "When you hear somebody that's hatin' on you or talking negatively about you, instead of being defensive, look at yourself and ask yourself, 'Is it true?' Is there something I can learn from this person that is a critic of mine that is giving me this feedback that I don't like?'"

Is there any piece of the criticism that is true and can help you grow? Once I get through that step, if the person has bad intentions or is simply a literal hater without a positive reason to help me, I had to learn to understand that. Everybody has that once they reach a certain level—Olympic athletes, professional fighters get critiqued after losing a fight by people who have never been in a fight in their life.

There are always critics and haters. LeBron could send a bunch of people to college and take care of a bunch of kids and never get in any trouble, and he still has haters. I realized that if you're ever gonna reach a level of greatness and success, it comes with people who will criticize you and hate you. I used to internalize that and get angry. I would want to talk to my haters because I would take it so personally. Now, I have a bunch of haters and still get eight hours of sleep, where before I couldn't sleep a wink.

Get comfortable as you elevate....there's a percentage of people who will hate you for whatever you do. They hated Jesus.

Deantè: *You are so correct. There is a perception that we have to be confident to achieve difficult things. I believe courage is more important than confidence. What experiences come to mind when you were afraid to try something because you lacked self-belief?*

Simon: Starting my business took courage. Moving to Pittsburgh, my mom quit her job, and it took her a long time to find a good job to where she was actually able to support the family and do things she wanted to do. For me, taking that risk at twenty-four years old took courage because I was a little scared, but I've heard you should *starve your fears and feed your focus*. I knew the focus was there, and I believed more than I feared, and I learned a lot of that through playing sports. To make an interception, you have to take a risk and go for the ball. As I got older, I began to notice more that people act like they have no fear. I was afraid walking into my first Ju-Jitsu gym when I started training over ten years ago. It's awkward—I never had professional training or any grappling or MMA experience, so I was walking into an uncomfortable environment. I think the hardest part for people who want to get into martial arts is just getting over the hump and walking in the damn door.

I was scared to get married. Then, I was like, "Man, what the hell took me so long?" I was with the same woman for over five years. I looked at my past experiences with family members and people I looked up to, and the majority either weren't married or had failed marriages and multiple divorces. So, I had that fear of "I don't want that to be me, so I'm just gonna avoid this situation and I don't even wanna hear the word *marry*." There will always be a risk to any greatness, but you have the pen in your hand and you can write the rest of the story to your book—and it's not determined by others. You're the author of the book that you're currently writing.

I learned that fear is a part of something you need to get over to take yourself to the next level in almost anything great. I always tell young people that to have big rewards, you typically have to take some risk, and I think that the best risk you could ever take is betting on your damn self. Players want to steal second base in baseball, but the only way to do that is by taking their foot off first base. But many people won't because they're so scared they will be thrown out at second, so they never make it around the damn bases.

That's what I learned about fear.

Deantè: *What advice would you give someone who is afraid to try because they are afraid to fail?*

Simon: Do it anyway. If you're scared to try because you're afraid to fail, you must force yourself to just show up that first day to get the first step started. Some people become paralyzed when analyzing, waiting, and calculating, but take that first step and understand that almost everybody has some form of fear. Watch the video of Mike Tyson where he talks about being scared to death when he was on his way to the ring. He said he had dreams of his opponents beating him and killing him, but the closer he gets to the ring, the more confident he becomes. Once he stepped into the ring, he felt a certain way.

Understand that at one point, Tyson was called "The Baddest Man on the Planet." He was one of the most feared men on the planet, and here he is talking about how he experienced fear on the way to his job—that's the job he chose to do, and nobody was forcing him to do it. He chose to go in the ring and fight with another man for no reason on a Wednesday. So, he was saying, "Even though I'm on my way to the job I chose, I'm still scared, but I do it anyway."

So, understand that courage isn't the absence of fear; it's being afraid and doing it anyway. And the more you "do it anyway," you'll realize that you ain't gonna die most of the time; you'll come back. In America, business owners have protections that aren't available in other countries. If your business fails or if you fail, it sucks, but we have bankruptcy here. You can file for bankruptcy and start over. You don't have to go to jail or become a slave for the next twenty years.

You'll learn that if you try a sport like boxing, the first time you get punched in the face, you're like, "Damn. I didn't die. I thought I was gonna die, but I didn't die, and it didn't hurt as bad as I thought." So, I think it's about learning to take action and control your emotions that cause fear. Everyone has fear and will continue to have fear when trying different things. You may have overcome fear in one area of your life, but if you want to get to the next level, you will encounter different fears and need to overcome those.

10.
JULIUS CHISHOLM:
IF YOU'RE NOT FIGHTING, YOU'RE BEING KILLED

Personal Trainer, Online Wellness Entrepreneur/3 years in business

Julius Chisholm would be among the greatest thinkers of any era, past or present, because his appetite for knowledge is insatiable. Simply referring to him as a trainer would be like referring to the Eiffel Tower as just a building or a Lamborghini as just a car. I'm amazed at the depth of his intellect and thought-provoking ideas because they carry lessons either simple or profound. It is my privilege to present to you Julius Chisholm.

—D.Y.

Deantè: *Based on your life experiences, how important has failure been to your success?*

Julius: Let's backtrack a little bit. When I was young, I was ignorant, meaning that I didn't know what failure was. And I'm not bashing school systems or governments or jobs, but they teach that failure is the worst thing on earth. When students and employees are conformed like that, they believe, "Oh, I can't fail at anything" and "Failure's bad," causing them to not take action.

When I was 25 or so, I thought, "This failure stuff sucks," and "I'm not getting anywhere." It was horrible, but now at age 32 I look at failure as "I'm looking to fail a lot more." As Inky Johnson says, "Perspective is key." Now that I have a different take on failure, I'm ecstatic.

I've failed many times in my life, and I'm like, "This is awesome" because now I know that the faster I fail, the faster I fall forward. If I hadn't failed, I wouldn't think like this. You wouldn't even be talking to me now.

Deantè: *Are you saying that failure has been absolutely essential to your success?*

Julius: Failure has put me in a position where if I never failed, I wouldn't be married today or pursuing business, entrepreneurship and success at the highly intensive rate that I am now.

Failure taught me to take responsibility for my actions, pursuits, dreams, and goals to break generational curses or just change the map in my own family. Many people are fighting that right now without understanding that it's a psychological thing. I've watched how much my family has failed in many areas, so comparing my failures to others allowed me to accept failure as a good thing instead of a negative thing.

Look at a kid who plays sports in middle school and misses the last shot or doesn't do well. They have a parent who doesn't know how to respond to failure because they're too busy living through their child. The parent wasn't bold enough, man or woman enough to achieve something, so that child developed a negative outlook on failure. When that student graduates, he's going to take the safe route, go to college and get a good job, and he's not going to try to not fail at anything because his parents never tried to achieve anything for fear of failing. He's going to fret, worry, and probably have a bad day.

Deantè: *Can the trickle-down effect of what you see in your environment during your formative years lead to a diminished belief in yourself?*

Julius: Yep. It's the perception of how people look at failure. If everybody looked at it as a good thing (the way that the most successful people do), people would try so much more. You can allow failure to cage you in, limiting your talents and stopping your potential and momentum.

That's if you look at failure the wrong way. If you look at failure as a vehicle, would you rather drive a Pinto or a Ferrari?

Deantè: *I would have a miscarriage in the Ferrari at this point, but I'd rather drive the Ferrari.*

Julius: And why would you rather drive the Ferrari?

Deantè: *Because it's higher class, more exclusive, it's sleeker, and quite frankly, it articulates your position in life.*

Julius: Well, I'll tell you how I look at the Pinto and how I look at the Ferrari. And this is how people look at failure. When they look at it in a negative light, they see it as a Pinto. The bad thing about a Pinto, even though it's temporarily reliable, it's horrible and outdated. It's slow, doesn't have a GPS, and nobody has to teach you how to drive it. But you have to keep buying more Pintos to get what you want, and you waste so much time constantly switching Pintos that you never get results when you want.

But a Ferrari is fast, mechanically gorgeous, has wonderful aesthetics, a GPS, and probably has seat warmers and coolers. It's not necessarily a more comfortable drive because you still have to learn how to drive the car. But you usually only have to buy one Ferrari, and you can move faster and get to the end goal faster. And the things that go into that Ferrari, I have to be a better-quality driver, it has to have better quality oil, it has to have a better-quality fuel—everything must be better, including the driver.

Deantè: *That's so profound! Especially because poverty-stricken people are always looking for the cheapest fuel to put in their car. You can't do that with a Ferrari, and if you are doing it with a Ferrari, you shouldn't have it.*

Julius: You definitely can't do that with a Ferrari. If you can't afford the maintenance, you shouldn't have the car. Let's convert that back to failure. If I'm afraid to fail, then I'm not willing to invest money into buying quality fuel, and I don't want the comforts of life. I don't want the cooling seats, and what you said about poverty—poverty is nothing but a mindset.

Deantè: *Would you say that's true for everybody, or is it just a select group of people where that's just a mindset and not a reality?*

Julius: Poverty is a mindset amongst everyone. I don't care if you make a million dollars a year, if you're just holding on to your money and hoarding it—poverty is restriction—it's called "playing it safe." But playing it safe is not the safest route; the safest route is going all in. You can't have an impoverished mindset that's holding you back.

Deantè: *When you say that poverty is everyone, are you speaking about people who are actually poverty stricken or are you talking about literally everyone?*

Julius: I'm talking literally. Poverty is a mindset.

Deantè: *Winning usually requires a lot of trial and error. What were some of your biggest challenges to get where you are now on your journey so far?*

Julius: My biggest challenge? You're looking at it. You are staring at the biggest challenge I have ever had in my life.

Deantè: *This is gold!*

Julius: This is not an arrogant statement: no one can beat me. You might be taller, cuter, more talented, grew up in a better neighborhood, and your mom might have a college fund for you—but you can't beat me.

Deantè: *But you can.*

Julius: I can smoke me! That can be taken as good or bad, and all my adversity has come from Julius, his decisions, his mindset, and how he thinks about things. Julius defeated Julius.

Deantè: *This is amazing because I have said that plenty of times, but not in this way. It sounds like arrogance, but it's quite the opposite; it's self-accountability.*

Julius: Every single situation in your life will tie back to you and your decisions.

Deantè: *How do you overcome being your biggest challenge?*

Julius: If you're going to take action on something and you feel resistance, you know you're on the right track. Your mind tries to keep you safe; poverty is supposedly safe, right? I always tell myself that I'm in control; I say, "You're my body, and I control you." I tell my mind what to think and what to do. I know I am doing the right thing if I feel fear or anxiety. We take these emotions that pop up as bad, negative, or dangerous, but you have to flip it on yourself and know that you're not doing anything illegal or wrong. You know the action is right, so you should do it.

The more you battle that danger or the "I'm not enough" signal is how you know you should do it. The way you should speak to yourself is to ask yourself, "Who's in control?" and "Who's are you?" When I'm in a good and spirited mood, I know I am a king of kings. I wasn't made to live with an impoverished mindset; I wasn't made to be limited or not to accomplish what I want to accomplish. I wasn't made to lose a battle that I have already won. So, if I already know those things about myself, and I know I am a conqueror, king, winner, and a giver, who am I to stop my physical self from winning?

Deantè: *What experience comes to mind when you were afraid to try something because you lacked self-belief or thought you would fail?*

Julius: Before my short stint in bodybuilding, I had the mentality of "I'm not good enough to be on stage yet." Even though I've been doing this for fourteen years, I'm still not good enough. Even though I've put in over 10,000 hours of intentional practice, making my body better, getting stronger, getting wiser in the fitness realm, I still felt like I wasn't enough. It prolonged me getting into bodybuilding, and I could've been on stages a long time ago.

Deantè: That's amazing. Even though you had fourteen years, had done above the work, you still had a negative self-image, probably because of the societal perception that you have to be this and that and that and this...

Julius: Yup. But guess who told me that I wasn't enough. Me. Everybody else kept telling me that I was enough.

Deantè: And your voice is the one that ultimately wins.

Julius: There are some people that come up in the world and you tell them your dreams and they say, "Naw that ain't gonna happen. Just stay safe and get a job...just go to school or go to the military...." I've never had anyone like that in my life that I recall. No one has ever told me I can't do something.

Deantè: How old were you when you went out for bodybuilding, and you had those doubts?

Julius: I was twenty-nine.

Deantè: That is super recent. And it's remarkable because it doesn't seem like something that you would let wrestle you to the ground mentally, even if you were thinking it.

Julius: I have a really close friend that would always tell me, "Man, Julius, you got it, you look great, you're always lean, this will be easy for you," and I was always saying I wasn't ready. But it gets to a point where you're fed up. The whole "not ready" thing is out the window. I'm done with that, and I *am* ready. And even if I'm not ready, I'm still going to do it.

Mark Batterson has a phenomenal quote. Ever hear "Ready, set, go?" People try to get ready and prepped, and then get set and bunched up...then they go. Mark Batterson says, "Go, set, ready," and what he means by that is just go and do it. You'll be set up, and by the time you're finished, you'll be ready. But you're already into the action because "Ready, Set, Go" is called procrastination.

People get ready, to get ready, to get ready, to get ready, to get ready, to get ready, to never get set, then they never go.

Deantè*: That's kinda what you were doing...*

Julius: Yep, I was. Until you have that break and say, "I'm doing this. I'm ready."

Deantè*: I'm actually glad to hear this because some people that we look at as being larger than life or always on and having it together, we need to hear the stories of the tribulations. Without those stories, it's hard for us sometimes to feel like we can do stuff that someone else can do because we think that they just automatically walked into greatness.*

Julius: No one wants to hear about the story of the guy who succeeded the first time.

Deantè*: What advice would you give someone who is afraid to try because they are afraid to fail?*

Julius: I don't want them to try anything. I want them to *do* something. Let's start there. I would pull out a notebook, get a wonderful pen to write with, and say to them, "Tell me what you *don't* want." Let's talk in the realm of finances and they are afraid to make them better. So, they make a long list of what they don't want to happen financially. Then, I tell them to pretend they are old and look again at those things they don't want to happen and understand that they're going to happen if they don't take action.

I don't want people to feel guilty, but they will feel like garbage when they don't try what they want. Do you really wanna sit with the thought of having not accomplished anything? Do you really wanna struggle and worry about money all the time? Do you really wanna be overweight and struggle going up stairs? Do you really wanna be a slave to your employer your whole life and make just 40K per year?

You're always going to be in the fight; that's the fun part. Nothing gets easier; you just get so much stronger that things look easy to you now. The 400 meters you ran did not get easier; it's still hard. But you're so conditioned and mentally and physically ready for that obstacle that it's easy now; it's a breeze. Once you get to that level of competency, start adding things, and getting stronger and more competent. It's always going to be a fight, who cares? Fight the fight; it doesn't matter.

I'd rather be fighting than dying. If you're not fighting, you're being killed.

11.
JONATHAN CHURCH:
SUFFER TODAY SO WE CAN CONQUER TOMORROW

Personal trainer | Fitness coach | successful Ju-Jitsu competitor | 3 years in business

Jonathan Church is almost psychopathic in the way he coaches people in the gym. He has a quick trigger, is demanding and impatient with his clients' excuses while training them, yet he has their full respect. Why is Church such an effective fitness coach? Because he only demands from others what he demands of himself. His success in Ju-Jitsu is proof that he walks the walk. It is my privilege to present to you Jonathan Church.

—D.Y.

Deantè: *Based on your life experiences, how important has failure been to your success?*

Jonathan: Without failure, there's no growth, so you need to fail to grow. For example, when I was competing, if I had never lost, I wouldn't have gotten better. I would've never seen my flaws or been able to grow from those flaws.

Deantè: *What type of competing do you do?*

Jonathan: I compete in Brazilian Ju Jitsu.

Deantè: *Is there a certain mindset that you must have with Ju Jitsu to keep you locked in the moment?*

Jonathan: I'm very competitive, so it's different from the regular Joe Schmo just going to practice or learning self-defense. I use it for sports...an outlet I guess you can say. Instead of going to practice once a week to learn how to properly defend myself, I go to learn how to win in competition.

Deantè: *Winning usually requires a lot of trial and error. On your journey so far, what were some of your biggest challenges to get to where you are right now?*

Jonathan: Probably becoming more dedicated. When I was younger, I made the same mistakes many young people make—going to parties, drinking a little bit too much, hanging out with the wrong crowd. So, once I dedicated myself, I started moving towards my goals on a real level. Anybody can look at you and say they want to do this and that, but then they don't put forth the effort. Many people are talkers; I'm not a talker.

My goal is to be a world champion, so I'm putting everything towards that goal. I enjoy and love combat sports. I started boxing when I was 12, and then I started wrestling. I wrestled for about seven or eight years and that led me to MMA. I grew up around my dad, who only boxed, so I thought about boxing, but once I started wrestling, other doors started opening. That's when I fell in love with Ju Jitsu because I thought wrestling was the best thing ever.

Ju Jitsu is pretty much wrestling on steroids.

Deantè: *Combat sports is something that you love. Does your dedication to it make it easier for you to overcome the challenges?*

Jonathan: Yes, because without any challenges, success won't be as sweet. If you go into a tournament or a fight and you obliterate your competition in a minute, that's one feeling. But if you win a really hard-fought fight and you get that medal or that belt, you sit back and think, "I did really good." It wasn't just an easy win; it wasn't just a guy who wasn't taking you seriously and you beat some bum.

So, without that challenge, it won't feel as good when you win.

Deantè: *You're never worried about getting hurt? The whole point of it is to destroy each other, right?*

Jonathan: Yeah.

Deantè: *I would be terrified. You're not worried about--*

Jonathan: No. I train really hard with really good fighters and competitors. So, it's part of it. I tore my bicep tendon, but it didn't happen during a match. Getting hurt and having bumps and bruises is all part of the game. No fighter in history has avoided getting hurt.

Deantè: *Do you need more of a mental toughness or physical toughness?*

Jonathan: Mental. You could be strong, fast, and explosive, but if you're mentally weak, you'll break under pressure. Once it gets hard, you'll quit.

Deantè: There is a perception that we must be confident to achieve difficult things. I believe courage is more important than confidence. What experience comes to mind in which you were afraid to try something because you lacked self-belief or didn't think you could do it?

Jonathan: I had that problem. Of course, going into a competition…. you're going to be nervous and anxious. There will be a little voice in your head saying, "What happens if I lose?" or "What happens if I can't do this?" You have to overcome that and have the courage to do it. You need the courage to go out of your way to ask for help.

It might've been hard to ask for help at first. It can be embarrassing to some people's mindset or thought process, but you need courage. Of course, your confidence will increase by doing it. You don't just wake up one day and you're good at something. You could have natural talent, but to be truly good or great at something, you must put in hard work. Without hard work or effort, you won't be good or great at anything.

Deantè: Do you ever doubt yourself now?

Jonathan: No. I let that go a long time ago. I'm a confident person as it is, but I have people relying on me because I have a family, so I can't have a negative mindset. You can have a negative mindset or a positive mindset, there's no "in between." You choose what mindset you're going to have. So, if I wake up and I say, "I can do this," and I'm positive about it, will it be difficult? Absolutely it's going to be hard; nothing in life is easy. But you have to choose that mindset. Of course, you will have bad days, causing you to second guess yourself, but that's part of the process.

Believe in yourself and work towards something that deep down you know--not think, you can do.

Deantè: *This is related to when you told me the difference between being driven and being motivated.*

Jonathan: Let's say that you're a huge football player, and watching a football game motivates you. Then you get a spot on a semi-pro team, play two games, and quit. Why did you quit? The motivation ran out, right? You're not motivated like that anymore. To be driven is to feel like that 24/7. It's not a want. It's "I need to reach my goal. I need it for me, I need it for my family because, after I reach my goal, that will open up other doors for myself in business or competition."

Be driven, not just motivated. Motivation goes away—drive doesn't.

Deantè: *What advice would you give someone who is hesitant to try because they are afraid that they might fail?*

Jonathan: Failure's a part of it. Let's look at some of the most successful people in the world. For example, how many times did Donald Trump fail? But he's not remembered for his failures; he's remembered for what he's done. Muhammad Ali. He's lost, right? Do you remember Muhammad Ali because he lost? No, you remember him because he's the greatest of all time, in his time, right?

Floyd Mayweather grew up with absolutely nothing. We know Floyd Mayweather from all the winning, the cars and all the money, but he lost earlier. He failed at the Olympics; he didn't get gold.

So, failure will happen. My advice to anyone who is scared to try something because they feel like they will lose or fail at it or just not succeed: You must at least try to do it because you're never going to do it unless you try. I can't decide to not write a book because I'm scared that it won't do well. If I don't write it, how will I know?

There's two ends to that. You're either going to fail or you're going to succeed, but that's on you. Eight and a half times out of ten, if a person gives their all to something, it's going to turn out positive for them. Even if it turns out negative and they fail, they don't feel like they failed because they tried their best. They put in the work and said, "I'm just gonna do it again," and they succeed the next time.

It's not how many times you get knocked down; it's how many times you get up. Everybody's heard that saying, and it's the truth.

12.
HONORÉE CORDER:
There's Always a Way if You're Committed

Author of 53 bestselling books | Strategic Book Coach | Owner of Honorée Enterprises Publishing | 17 years in business

Honorée Corder is a powerhouse in the publishing industry and has successfully built an empire that uplifts other writers to hopefully follow in her footsteps. But despite her significant success, Honorée is the most down-to-earth, funny, and genuine person that you'll meet. Her generosity and unrelenting passion to pursue her goals are two of her greatest qualities. It is my privilege to present to you Honorée Corder.

—D.Y.

Deantè: Based on your life experiences, how important has failure been to your success?

Honorée: I don't use the "F" word. There are other "F" words that I use, as you know. I think you either win or you learn, so I turn failure into learning. Failure has been very instrumental in my success because you miss 100% of the shots you don't take, and I've taken a lot of shots. Of course, I've had some singles, doubles, and home runs; but I've also had several things knock me back giving me an opportunity to ponder and reflect, do better and try again.

So, I think it's been instrumental, but not in the way others might think about it. They might think, "Well, you have to fail so many times before you succeed." I've always chosen to look at failure as a learning opportunity and a chance to maybe slow my roll a little bit or take stock of what I did win out of the situation and how I benefitted. All the time, I believe rejection is protection, so when I haven't succeeded at something, I've been redirected, and that's resulted in a failure.

Deantè: Just to clarify, when I say "failure," I'm speaking about society's perspective on what's considered failure.

Honorée: How do you think society views failure?

Deantè: I think society views it as if you don't achieve what you tried to do, you've failed, even though it's a learning experience and it's essential because when you "fail" you do learn. Your life is better anyway because you had to become a certain type of person once you went through that process.

Honorée: Yes! I think if you've had to work hard for something, you appreciate when something *does* work. I am eternally grateful; I never take anything for granted and I never stop working hard. Because I've had my share of failures, setbacks, challenges, hardships, and heartbreaks, I appreciate every person, every dollar, and every moment more than I would have if it had all been easy. If it had come to me easily, I probably wouldn't appreciate it as much.

Deantè: You are correct on that. Next question: winning usually requires a lot of trial and error. On your journey so far, what were some of your biggest challenges to get you to where you are right now?

Honorée: I had a tough upbringing. I spent some time in foster care and lived in a children's home, so I did not have the white picket fence or an intact, loving family unit that we would all like to have. I did not go to college, and for a long time everybody asked, "Where did you go to school?" In other words, "Where did you get your higher education?" I never acquired a traditional higher education, so that was a challenge. Then, I went through a divorce in my early 30s and I was a single mom. I've had a number of books that didn't do as well as I wanted. Sometimes I would think, "Oh, this book is going to be the book that hits and does the best and makes the best impact," and nothing happened.

And then sometimes I write something and go "mmm" and it seems to hit a chord. Go figure. There have been different businesses and different things that I have engaged in that worked for a while and then stopped working. I've had my fair share of challenges that have taught me to be resilient and to keep showing up. I just keep showing up.

Deantè: How many books do you have published?

Honorée: Fifty-three.

Deantè: Yeah. That's a lot of learning.

Honorée: I know.

Deantè: What experience comes to mind when you were afraid to try something because maybe you lacked belief in yourself or you didn't think you could actually achieve it?

Honorée: I had people tell me from a young age that based on my background, I could have gotten scholarships, grants, or loans, but I didn't know what to do. I was afraid I would do it wrong, so I never did it. I definitely had the opportunity, and I didn't take it. Who knows what I missed out on because of that?

Deantè: Well, think about what we would have missed out on if you didn't go down this path.

Honorée: Thank you. That's very kind. I don't know what would've happened had I gotten a traditional education. I don't regret it; Deantè, don't get me wrong. I'm very happy where I sit. I wake up every day and say, "They still haven't come for me." I wake up and have a job to go to, right? So I feel lucky every single day I wake up. Every single morning, I wake up and say, "Okay, still here, still doin' it, let's go."

Deantè: Yeah, it seems like the universe didn't want you to go down that path because think about how many people's lives you've impacted. Not just me, but Hal (Elrod) and many other people, so that's a plus.

Honorée: That's very humbling to think about, but that's why I do what I do—to make an impact. The reason I still do what I do every day is because I absolutely love it and I get to have conversations like this one.

Deantè: Well, I appreciate that, and we do have that Ohio connection so that's another thing.

Honorée: We do, yes! Buckeyes!

Deantè: *What advice would you give someone who is afraid to try because they are afraid that they might fail? You know, try something that they might really wanna accomplish whether it's a dream, a goal or something that might even be their destiny?*

Honorée: You will only regret what you don't do. There are very few things that you will attempt to do even if you don't succeed or don't fulfill the picture in your mind, that you'll regret. I look back over my life and the things I regret are the things I didn't do, not the things I did. Even the mistakes or what could be considered mistakes, I don't regret those because they informed and influenced what happened later.

But the things that I didn't do, I think, "Oh! I really should've just done that," and I didn't. Now, the time has passed, and you never get that time back. And boy does it go by fast.

13.
ASA COX:
THERE'S NO SUCH WORD AS NO

Owner of Asa's Homes Century 21 | Owner of Asa's Angels | 30+ years in business

Asa Cox is one of the most compassionate, giving people that I've ever met. She is mostly unimpressed with her own extraordinary success in business because she cares most about helping others in need. Her impoverished upbringing and endless challenges in her early life greatly inspire the limitless charitable endeavors that she creates to help and heal her community. It is my privilege to present to you Asa Cox.

—D.Y.

Deantè: Based on your life experiences, how important has failure been to your success?

Asa: Very important. I was married at 13 years old, and we were very poor. We lived on North State Street in Painesville, Ohio, which is one of the lower-income housing areas. My mom and I rented from my uncle and paid $150 a month. My dad died three months before I was born, so it was pretty much just me and my mom most of the time. She did get married, so I had a stepdad along the way, but they got divorced. So, when I met my husband at age 13, our car had broken down on the road and he pulled up on a motorcycle and fixed it for us. It was a hundred-dollar car; I'll never forget it.

I fell in love with him after he fixed the car and married him. We've been married 44 years now. I attended Harvey High School in Painesville, and I hated school. I would only go for one or two classes, and I carried a "D" average all the way from 13 until my husband made me graduate at 18.

At that point, I decided to do something with my life, and I had no money for college—we could barely pay rent. When I was 20, I looked into buying a house because I'd heard the housing market was great. My stepfather at the time gave us the small down payment that we needed. When we bought the house, the realtor told me that I would be great in real estate sales because I was so mature for my age.

That comment encouraged me to consider going to school for real estate, and it changed my whole life. Remember, I had no college experience. Real estate school was only a six-week course, and I ended up getting my real estate license. I figured there had to be a way that someone could help a person like myself who had no college and made very small income.

I learned about a program called USDA, which came directly from the government. I connected people with USDA to get a loan, including my daughter who bought her house for $25 at 18 years old making $12 per hour. She bought a $164,000 house for $600 a month. I really wanted to change lives one at a time because I knew there were people making ten or twelve dollars per hour that could never afford a home, and I wanted to help them.

That led to me starting my charity, *Asa's Angels*. Even though I have made money in my career, I still live in my $77,000 house that we bought years ago. I decided to give my money to the community in which I grew up.

Deantè: On your journey so far, what have been the biggest challenges to get to where you are right now?

Asa: A lot of people in the community say, "Don't work with her because she works with people who are no good and don't have money. She works with poor things; her programs are not true." I hear on a daily basis, "Should I list with you? I heard that you only work with poor people." My response to that is that it doesn't matter how much money you make, it matters how you decide to use that money. My challenges are every day; they don't stop at real estate and business. I want to make sure I use my voice to the community so others can help, because if it wasn't for my voice, we wouldn't get as much in.

Keep in mind, it's not me because the people don't donate to me.

Deantè: What experience comes to mind when you were afraid to try something because you lacked self-belief?

Asa: I bring so many realtors on and train them so they can go from working in a bar making $10,000 a year to working on my team making $100,000 a year. Then, they leave and start their own teams in the industry because they've learned everything from me.

They wear me down every day and take everything I've taught them to start their own group. That's probably my hardest thing on a daily basis. I want to bring people in and work with them on the company side, but as soon as I do and they're making $100,000 plus a year, they want $200,000 a year.

Deantè: *Does that type of betrayal make you gun shy about trying with people?*

Asa: Absolutely. I get calls from people who want to join the company, but I don't want to bring them in because I'm afraid they're going to do that to me again.

Deantè: *What advice would you give someone who is afraid to try something because they are afraid to fail?*

Asa: I'd tell them that they have nothing to lose, but they do have something to gain potentially. If they don't try, they're not going to win, so they should always try because their time is priceless.

14.
WAYNE DAWSON:
THE SEEDS OF GREATNESS ARE WITHIN YOU

Anchor/Reporter for Fox 8 News | Pastor at Grace Tabernacle Church | 40 years in business

Wayne Dawson has become such an indelible staple of news reporting in Northeast Ohio, that I consider him to be a member of my family. Beneath his excellent presence on local television, Wayne's love for his family, faith in God, and phenomenal determination to achieve greatness are what defines him. He is candid, generous, tough as nails, and very funny. It is my privilege to present to you Wayne Dawson.

—D.Y.

Deantè: Based on your life experiences, how important has failure been to your success?

Wayne: You know, failure is never fun. It's something that can sap your confidence if you allow it. But I believe failure is a necessary part of your journey to success. I've failed several times, but I still try to find something I can use or learn from the experience. I always say that every failure, every defeat, every setback carries with it the seed or equivalent of a greater comeback.

The key to failures in life is to learn from those. Look at them and figure out what you did wrong. Ask yourself, "How can I change that?" Try to learn everything you can from the situation, but then bury it. You can't dwell on it; you gotta keep it moving.

If you keep thinking about your failures, you're prone to repeat them.

Deantè: *I would definitely agree with that. A lot of people think failure is a bad word, but when I say "failure," I'm really talking about society's perception of what failure is. Meaning, if you don't achieve something that you set out to do, then you've failed. In reality, it's all a teaching tool.*

Wayne: It's totally a teaching tool. And that's why anyone who's successful in life has failed time and time again; it's part of the learning process. The difference between the individual who succeeds and one who does not is how they deal with failure, setbacks, defeats, and disappointments.

As I said before, just keep moving and study it. What did you do right? What did you do wrong? How can you approach this a little bit differently next time? If you can learn from it, you can use it as a steppingstone to greater success. Also, if you study the lives of successful individuals, that's what they do. They don't allow failure to bury them. They emerge from their failure better, stronger, and more focused, and that's what you have to do. When you realize that, failure is never fatal...unless you allow it to be.

And if you realize failure is part of their journey to success, you'll have a better mindset when you deal with a situation where you're not as successful as you'd like to be the first time, or if you fail.

Deantè: *I cannot agree more. Now, winning usually requires a lot of trial and error. On your personal journey so far, what were some of your biggest challenges to get where you are now?*

Wayne: From the latter part of my teen years, I was the product of a single-parent household. I lived with my mom, and we were on welfare living in East Cleveland. That city wasn't as bad as it is now, but it was still pretty challenging. I'm not proud of it, but I did drugs and barely made it through high school. Not because I couldn't do it, but because I just had no interest in doing the work.

I did the bare minimum to get by and almost fell into a situation where I would've been a statistic. I probably wouldn't have had a good job or could've ended up in jail. So that's where I started out and it was a challenging situation...and on top of that, I was a teenage parent. I came from a pretty difficult environment, and I was able to escape it mainly because of the individuals that the Lord put in my life.

The Lord put someone in my life at that particular time who helped me pull out of it. He was a basketball player at Shaw High School, and he said, "Wayne, let me tell you...I'm gon' make the NBA, and in 10 years you'll be doing the same thing you're doing: getting high and hangin' out with them guys. You ain't gon' be doing nothin'. You really need to go to school, and I'm going to Tri-C and I'm gon' play ball."

He convinced me to enroll in Tri-C, and remember, I wasn't thinking about college at that time, but I did it. That changed my life around and I became interested in my education. It was a situation where I could've gone one way or the other, and like I said, the Lord has guided my life by putting people in my path to help guide me in the direction that He wanted me to go.

Now, it was up to me to take advantage of the situation. Just because these people were in my life and telling me to go to school, that could've gone the other way. Despite what I went through and coming from a typical Black situation, inner city kind of stuff, I was the first one in my family to graduate college. And even though I was in that situation, I always felt that I could do better for some reason. Deep down inside, I knew that I could make something of myself. That and my mother's prayers kept me going.

Deantè: *I always believe that the people who are able to last are the ones who succeed no matter what because they endure so many trials and tribulations. My grandmother always talked about overcoming trials and tribulations and spoke often about God. She said, "When God is for you, He's more than the world against you."*

Wayne: Yes. There's no doubt about that. My mom's prayers were very prevalent in my life and my brother's life because we both came from the same situation. Another challenge was being able to focus as a single parent, knowing I wanted to be a good parent, but also wanting to go to school and make something of myself. Fortunately, I had a girlfriend at the time who was in my corner and really helped me out in that situation by allowing me to go to school and not pressuring me to do whatever.

Another challenge was when I started at Fox 8. It's crazy how I got there, but once I got there, they told me that I had a "black dialect." I was told, "You need to straighten out that black dialect," and I asked, "What are you talking about? This is the way I talk." So, they paid for me to attend a speech class at Case

Western to help me get rid of my "black dialect" and I was saying to myself, "This is crazy!" But I guess it worked. I still have a black dialect, and I think that's a good thing, but just being able to overcome...I wasn't like most of the black guys that got into TV, even today. Most black guys in TV today come from middle-class backgrounds—most brothas in TV today on air didn't come from the inner city. They didn't come from the hood; they come from middle-class and upper middle-class backgrounds, integrated societies and all of that.

But I came from 105th, Drexel, East Cleveland. So, I'm a different kind of guy, and I'm proud of it, ya know? But coming from that space and being able to negotiate in the space I'm in now, is something I've had to learn how to do. Because I'm black through and through—and there's a lot of brothas who are black on the outside, but they ain't black on the inside—especially in television, so I'm a brotha through and through, and proud of it.

Deantè: *When I'm watching you on television, I can tell that you have that flair. We see it in Arsenio, we see it in Steve Harvey...*

Wayne: Yeah, and they're all from Cleveland, and we're in the same age category too. I went to college with Arsenio. He was at Kent when I was there, and I would see him in the music and speech room, but he didn't graduate. He left and went on to bigger and better things.

Deantè: *That's so awesome. What experience comes to mind when you were afraid to try something because you lacked self-belief or you didn't think you could accomplish it.*

Wayne: I'm gonna be honest with you: getting married. I just didn't think I could be a good husband because I had a lot of "playa" in me, ya know? I was always messin' around and never really serious about a relationship. So, as I was getting ready to be married, I thought, "Am I doing the right thing?" I was kinda fearful because I wasn't sure I could be committed. I wasn't sure I could be that guy that would always be there, so that was one of those situations where I was fearful, but I took the plunge and did it anyway.

And praise God, because He changed me from where I was to where I'm at now. That was a fearful step with coming from a single-parent household, remembering when my mom and dad were together and there was a lot of friction and fighting. So, I had that fear of commitment and getting married, but I guess my wife gave me an ultimatum and I said, "I guess I might as well do it." All the way up until the wedding day, I was like, "Do I really wanna do this?"

I must admit this: early on, I had relatives around me that instilled confidence in me, who told me to be proud to be black and kept instilling confidence in me. And so whatever situation I dealt with, I knew deep-down that I could deal with it and handle it. And that was because they spoke life into me. Even though I came from a less-than-desirable environment, my relatives—aunts, uncles, my mom especially—they just spoke life into me.

My brother and I started *The Annie L. Dawson Foundation* to honor our mom for speaking life into both of us. My brother is a judge in East Cleveland, the same city we grew up in, but my mother made us believe that there was nothing we could not accomplish if we put our minds to it. That's how I approach situations, so when I started preaching, it was a fearful situation because the pastor had been there for thirty years. When he died, they asked me to be the interim pastor, and eventually to be their regular pastor.

I had never pastored before, and I had no intention of being a pastor because I was an associate at my other church. I only started doing it because being on TV, churches would ask me to come do Men's Day stuff. If I was going to speak at the church, I figured I might as well learn a little bit about the Bible, so I started taking classes and one thing led to another. To make a long story short, I was fearful. I was like, "Can I do this?" I never pastored before and I really didn't know the word as well as probably a lot of people do, but I jumped in it anyway even though I wasn't that confident. I figured, "What the heck?" I did the best I could possibly do, so I overcame that fear, but there were a lot of fears. I believe fear is a vehicle of the enemy as well, and I think the devil likes to infiltrate our minds with negative thoughts and fearful thoughts like, "I'm not good enough, I can't do this, I can't do that." When God thinks you can do all things through Christ, it strengthens you. Much of my strength comes from my relationship with Christ, and my power comes from that power. In my own strength, I really can't do it. But with the strength of the Lord and the Holy Spirit in me, I can do all things.

I think God has always had His hand on my life because if you look at where I came from and the stuff I was up against, for me to be where I am today…it doesn't make any sense. But hey man, the key is this: it doesn't matter where you come from or how you start; it's how you finish. That's what people gotta understand. Just like you said, "Courage is more important than confidence."

Sometimes you don't have the confidence, and I know I didn't have it to say, "Okay, I'm gonna take over this church," but God gave me the courage to do it. So, when you don't have confidence, you have the courage and just jump in there, man. And if you jump in there with courage, the confidence will come.

When I first started at Fox 8, for some reason, I knew I could do it. I had the confidence for it, and I don't know why. At Kent State, I was the news director, and when I got to Fox 8, I was like, "Shoot, I can do this! I'm better than this person or that person!" I had the confidence for that, but when it came to the preacher thing, the church thing—it was a whole different ball game for me.

When I came to Fox 8, I knew I had prepared and had studied my craft. I'm typically a confident guy, so I was ready to roll. I probably thought I was better than I was, but when it came to the church, I just had to jump in there and do it, and it worked out okay. That's the message: just do it and don't be afraid to fail, which is the difference between success and ultimate failure.

Deantè: *What advice would you give someone who is afraid to try because they are afraid to fail?*

Wayne: You gotta do it. Jump in and don't be afraid. If you fail, so what? If you understand that failure is part of the process of achieving ultimate success, then do it and don't worry about it. I was watching a movie the other day, and one of the characters kept saying, "I failed the test, but I'ma take it again!" He came back and said the same thing a few times. No matter how many times you fail, just keep doing it and you will succeed. Like I said, the key is that you learn from it. Fail a test? Okay, let me go over the test and figure out what I did wrong. Don't be afraid of failure because it's part of success—everybody has failed; everybody that's ever achieved anything great in life has failed.

Look at Joe Biden, the president now, he failed twice running for president until he finally got elected. Everybody has failed, and it is what it is, but the key is how will you deal with it? Do you accept it and say, "Okay that's it, I failed once, I'm done." Or do you say, "Okay. Let me see how I can come at it another way?" Every setback is a setup for a comeback, but it's how *you* view it. If you view it in a negative way, then it is what it is. You gotta view it in a positive way, and that's where self-awareness comes in. You gotta know you can do it even if it takes longer than expected.

Deantè: *You are the epitome of that whole philosophy because like you said, you never thought that you'd get to this place considering how you started.*

Wayne: Yes. I'm talking from the experience that I have, and being a reporter, I've seen it in others. This is all a growing process and a molding process. Don't be defined by your failures; that's the key. Know that they are just stumbling blocks and you gotta get up, dust yourself off, and keep it moving. Ultimately, if you do that, you will reach your destination.

15.
EMIL GAMIDOV:
Failure is Fake

President and CEO of the ONYX 24-hour fitness franchise | 5 years in business

Emil Gamidov wants to take the world by storm in the future by laying a stainless-steel foundation of dedication in the present. He is that rare entrepreneur who achieves a lot but knows he can do so much more and will tirelessly work to make that vision a reality. Most business executives love the results of their efforts, but Emil is enthusiastic about the work required to get there. It is my privilege to present to you Emil Gamidov.

—D.Y.

Deantè: Based on your life experiences, how important has failure been to your success?

Emil: People look at failure like "It's taking me down to the ground floor," but most don't see the next step. The cool part about rock bottom is there's nowhere to go below that. So, once you hit rock bottom, it's the easiest place to bounce back from. I reached success at a very early age. After high school, I started working in the fitness industry, and when my friends went to college at 18 and 19, I was already a general manager at a health club facility, Bally's Total Fitness, running a multi-million-dollar gym.

I bought my first house at 19, and had a Hummer, a motorcycle, and a boat. I remember visiting my friends in college and they were eating Ramen noodles. When I pulled up in my Hummer, they thought I was selling drugs, but I'm like, "Naw man, I'm working at a gym." By 24, I filed bankruptcy, then 2008 hit. Bally's started going through financial trouble and my lifestyle went from making over $100,000 a year to making $8 an hour.

My car got repossessed, my house was foreclosed, and I was going through a bad relationship that ended in a breakup. My rock bottom was when I lived in Lyndhurst, Ohio in a home with no electricity and water leaking from the second floor into my kitchen with the tub hanging down. I even hit depression for a few weeks wondering what I had gotten myself into. I didn't talk to my father, and his dream was for me to go to college.

He's a truck driver, so his sacrifice for us was in moving to the United States and getting me to finish college, get a job, work 40 or 50 years, and retire. When I dropped out of college, it hit him very hard, and it put a big wedge into our relationship. We didn't talk for three or four years, and at the time, I really felt alone. My mom lived in Europe and even though we talked on the phone, I kept things to myself.

I never told anyone about the hard times I was going through. I kept telling people that everything was great and to me, that was part of the positive talk in my mind, but in real life, I was not. I was laying on the couch with no job, everything was falling apart, and suddenly, I was offered an opportunity with Toshiba. That's when things started turning around for me because I was taking control of knowing what happened to me, where I was at, the success that I reached at such an early age, how it all fell apart, and then being able to rebuild that.

I feel that you need to go through failures to discover what success tastes like. You also need to have success to know what it tastes like and understand what you could possibly lose. It's a double-edged sword that you have to experience on both ends.

Deantè: *So, you became successful because of your failures, not in spite of them?*

Emil: Those failures started in school. I was never a studious kid. I wanted to play sports, and now when I look back at our school system, I think it fails a lot of people. It's one way of being taught, like a factory mindset. You raise your hand when you have to go to the bathroom, a bell rings at a factory line when you're done with your job, and that's how it relates back to the schooling.

So, a bell rings, you get up and go to the next class. When you graduate high school, they teach you how to build a resume, not how to build a business plan or how to get started for yourself. We are taught how to just go in the flow of everybody else. So if you're anything different from that, you're automatically classified as a failure. They don't know how to support you or different mindsets, so you're put in a category of not fitting the profile they want from 98% of people graduating.

When you're a kid, your parents have a similar mindset. They're employees, right? They're not entrepreneurs, so they also think that you're a failure. So, there's this crumbling world where you're the only one who has to believe in yourself and say, "No, I'm made for something different," even if you don't know what that is yet.

My failure came in high school. During my senior year, I picked up my cap and gown months before graduation. Then, my counselor told me that I wasn't graduating that year and I would have to go to summer school. My dad told me to go to trade school and said that I was obviously not trying to be successful. That was a hurtful time, but also a motivational time because I'm a person that wants to do things that others can't do, or something that others tell me can't be done.

After that conversation with my dad, I said to myself that I was going to graduate and to make it happen, and I literally went to an all-girls high school. I found a tutor to help me after school to get the credits I needed to graduate on time. I graduated on time with all my friends, and that was the first time I realized that when someone tells you it can't be done, it's not the only way.

You have 100% control of your life and where you're trying to go.

Deantè: *On your journey so far, what were some of the challenges to get where you are?*

Emil: When you're building something, you can't do it on your own. You need a team and people to believe in that vision. When you start building something worthwhile, you gotta know there will be challenges. One of my biggest challenges in building my organization is that we are the largest privately held fitness health club chain in Ohio with thousands of members in Northeast Ohio.

But that came with "I can't do that on my own." That came with building the right teams. Building the right team is the number one biggest challenge in any organization, sports team etc. It comes down to building the right team.

That entails having the right culture, vision, and mission statement to underline your company's beliefs and what it's striving to accomplish. It's a big challenge to get others to understand and see the vision.

People give up on themselves at the first sign of challenge or hardship, and I try to make people see their true potential. Sometimes in leadership, you bring people on, develop them, and they don't see what you see because you've experienced the failure, success, failure. You've seen people who you have mentored with the same pattern or structure, and sometimes you see more in them than they see in themselves.

You just wanna take your mind and give them a little chip and download it in their own head to see that same vision.

Deantè: Is there something that you see in a person that lets you know it's the right fit for you?

Emil: Teachability and coachability. If they're coachable, I feel like that's 90% of the way because they are willing to learn and willing to listen. You can be hardheaded or tough to manage, or you could be a superstar who knows your value and worth, that's all great and dandy.

But if you have that coachability and you're sitting there as a student to the game every single day, that's the number one characteristic any leader, manager ,or mentor is looking for in an individual they want to bring up.

Deantè: What experience comes to mind when you were afraid to try something because you lacked self-belief?

Emil: Where we're at right now; ONYX. Think about what we've accomplished so far. We are playing amongst Fortune 100 and Fortune 500 national companies out there. Planet Fitness spends millions of dollars per month on advertising and has thousands of locations. Anytime Fitness has 5,000 locations nationwide—they're one of the largest fitness chains…Snap Fitness, World's Gym, Gold's Gym.

And I said to myself, "We're going to play in that arena." We're going to compete with the national boys out there and go into their world and win. That was scary.

Deantè: Were you doubting it?

Emil: One hundred percent. Because when you're sitting there, you're doubting it can be done. I told myself I didn't have the funds, resources, or connections. I'm trying to beat Goliath. I'm trying to go into a lion's cage without any tools saying, "I'm gonna figure it out." It was very scary and very doubtful.

And that fear comes at every location that we open. I have three completed deals on my table waiting for my signature.

Deantè: Are you scared?

Emil: Scared. Nervous. Doubtful. Every single step of the way. If you listen to any athletes—Tom Brady, Floyd Mayweather—they always say that before every game or fight, they still get butterflies, still get the nervousness.

As soon as that goes away, something's wrong, and it's not keeping you on your toes. You're too comfortable, and that's where you lose. I'm always nervous, but I feel like the butterflies in my stomach keep me on my toes.

But then comes that self-confidence and awareness I talked about earlier. It comes where you're able to self-check and be self-aware. My inner voice is like, "You've done this now eight times. What's nine times? Why's it gonna be different? You have proved to yourself that your systems and processes work. You have proved you have the right people in place and you can be at the bottom and build yourself back up."

Always feel like "I don't care if I lose everything tomorrow, I know I can rebuild it the next day." I think that's the biggest confidence I have and the biggest support I have from my wife. When you're a leader, not only in your family, but in your business and in your community, when you put yourself out there, it puts a little different pressure on you. I remember my wife telling me she didn't care if we lived in a box as long as we're healthy and have food, and that gave me confidence.

I look at business and life almost like a game of Monopoly. If you and I played Monopoly every single day, you're going to get pretty good at it because you'd look at it as a game. So, I look at life as a game, and the better I am at playing this game and the more fun I have playing it, the more successful I'm going to be. If I lose this game, I'm going to start over and play a new game.

Deantè: *What advice would you give someone who is afraid to try because they are afraid to fail?*

Emil: I would first tell them that failure is self-applied in their mind. I would give them an example like, "If you tried riding this bike and you fail at it, what's the worst-case scenario? You're gonna fall, you're gonna get a scrape, you're gonna maybe bleed a little but you can just put a Band-Aid on it and get right back on." So, it's the whole concept that there's no such thing as failure—you're just learning what you did wrong and how you're going to make it different next time.

I think the worst failure is overplayed and it's almost fear. People are always like, "What's your biggest fear?" Failure! And I'm thinking, "What?" My biggest fear is death because I'm not going to be able to do it again tomorrow, so I don't want to not be doing something or wasting time. People who say they don't wanna try because they are afraid of failure are fake. Failure is fake. There's no such thing as failure. Failure is: *I tried something and it didn't work out because I made a mistake*.

Think about this: are you reinventing the wheel by writing a book?

Deantè: No.

Emil: Right. Millions of people before you wrote books. So, if you fail, who are you gonna look at? Yourself. So, there's no such thing as failure because it's a self-applied fake word. Sometimes, people are bad at self-awareness, like...I know that I'm not going to be the next Michael Jordan. I'm five-six, not as fast, and I don't have the moves. Since I know all that, I'm not going to position myself to be Michael Jordan. I know I won't be good at it.

I'm going to be self-aware and double down on something I am good at. People don't practice self-awareness and doubling down on what they're good at often enough. That goes back to playing Monopoly; the more you play it, the more you know if you're good at one aspect of it or another. Once you figure it out, you start making the right decisions and putting yourself in a position to win.

16.
AARON GREEN:
Tomorrow Starts Today

Owner and CEO, Elite Personal Fitness | Actor | 16 years in business

Aaron Green showed me two different sides to his personality. First, I saw the soft-spoken gentle giant who happens to be a dedicated man of faith. Then, I saw the ultra-intense, yet charismatic warrior who's built a thriving personal training business and a growing stream of acting credits. I admire his fondness for his family, as well as his resilience. It is my privilege to present to you Aaron Green.

—D.Y.

Deantè: *Based on your life experiences, how important has failure been to your success?*

Aaron: When facing failure, the strong people continue and the lesser ones just fail. If you're a strong individual who fails at something, you are not a failure. I can't stress that enough because my foundation is with Christ. When you have failure, you need someone in your corner to let you know you did not fail. My wife let me know that I did not fail. When I first started, I came home with a check from one client for fifty-five dollars. I handed it to my wife and said, "This is all I made this week." She looked at me and said, "I know you're gonna make this work."

So, when I failed, I had a support system right there. I don't know if she secretly cried her eyes out and regretted marrying me. But when she told me that she had the faith that I was going to make it work, that's all I needed. So that was my "failure."

Deantè: *Support systems are very important. Has her support helped your journey of failing? When I say "failing," I mean the public's perception of failure. Has it made it easier for you to take risks?*

Aaron: Yes. Ever since then, that person has been in my corner since day one...when I think things aren't going well, I know that someone believes in me. And that one person is all I need to succeed.

Deantè: *Winning usually requires a lot of trial and error. On your journey so far, what were some of your biggest challenges to get to where you are now?*

Aaron: First thing is trust. I go inside people's homes and that is their intimate domain. There's no funny business because people trust me, and trust is very important. So, everything I do is on the up and up. There's this whole crazy perception and some people react like, "Oh my gosh. A personal trainer is coming to your house! Is he cute?" None of that; it's all about staying professional because if you lose that trust, everything is out the window.

Deantè: *Has it been a challenge to get the trust from others?*

Aaron: No, because I come in honest and open and it's all about me making a person better and I've earned that trust. I tell people upfront that I don't walk on water, and I can't feed the multitudes. I'm only the catalyst and I don't live with them, so I can't slap that extra chicken bone out of their mouth. The plan is to get them where they want to go and reach their goals. If you're upfront with someone, there's trust right there.

Deantè: Is that a challenge to get your clients to follow what you're saying?

Aaron: Yes! But they know it. I've always found that you should surround yourself with people who are smarter than you, and the people I deal with are all extremely smart. Yes, they know what to do, but are they gonna do it? Maybe sometimes they'll do it and stop, but a lot of times, they know it's on them. It's on me to make sure they don't get hurt during the home workouts and everyone has their cross to bear. I can't force anything because the second that's done, you lose their trust, and trust is very important.

Deantè: There is a perception that we have to be confident in order to achieve difficult things. I believe courage is more important than confidence, so what experiences come to mind when you were afraid to try something because maybe you lacked belief in yourself?

Aaron: In 1999, I was wrongfully downsized from my job because they accused me of stealing. It took me a year and a half to find another job, even though I have a bachelor's degree and a major in Lit relations and a minor in human resource management. I worked at a trucking terminal, and was fired from it after a year and a half of looking for work and being turned down because I had too much experience, which sounded ludicrous to me. I was living in my grandma's basement, and I had a cousin who was a caregiver for a gentleman in lake county and he needed to get around.

I was told that he had a weight room and a pool, so I started training him, his secretary, and his daughter. Along the way, I was still getting turned down for jobs, and it really hurt me because I was told that the world is open to anyone with a degree. But I was still having fun training that group of people, and I also started working at the YMCA. Soon after that, I reached the end of training the group while also getting certified at the Y. I found another job, but soon was downsized from that one too. That failure was the eye opener that gave me confidence. When a person gets turned down enough, we tend to ask ourselves, "What do I like to do?" Sometimes, we gotta go to a dark place, and for me, that was my grandma's basement.

Asking myself what I liked doing, I realized that I liked people and exercise, and after getting downsized again, I went to the Cleveland Athletic Club and asked for a job. It just so happened that one of the trainers was leaving at the same time. So, I had to go through all that just to have the courage to walk in off the street and ask for a job. Once I got in, the confidence came along. So, I think it's courage first and then confidence.

Deantè: *Did hearing employers say that you were overqualified make you doubt yourself?*

Aaron: Yes, very much so. I was doubting myself big time and I even tried to convince the human resource manager. He straight up told me that I would leave them in six months. I said, "What if I don't leave? You don't know that because I might love it here." He told me that they couldn't take that risk, but I saw it as a risk/reward because they'd be hiring a solid individual.

Deantè: *What advice would you give someone who is maybe afraid to try because they are afraid to fail?*

Aaron: Not trying is failing, let's keep that simple. You will fail if you have not tried. You wanna ride a bike, get on a bike. Okay, you fall but you'll have your support group there to pick you up, so try it. Often, I think we put ourselves in cages when we don't allow ourselves to go outside the box. When comedians try different jokes and bomb, now they know that it didn't work, but at least they tried. We gotta keep trying and trying and trying, and if it doesn't work, that's when we gotta have that support system.

Whatever you do in life, your personality has to come out. If your personality can't come out, you are in a cage. While I was doing personal training, I felt like there was more I could do in life. I am charismatic and I love people, but I get shy around groups of people.

Once, I was cast in a movie. I had never been in a movie and the only acting I had ever done was as a stand-in for a LeBron James commercial years ago.

I showed up on the set because of my confidence and the belief that there was something more within me. I needed to branch out, and the next thing I knew, I was reading lines for the movie. I liked that the director challenged me, but on the first day of shooting, there was a scene that took us twenty-seven takes! I was struggling so bad with my lines that at the seventeenth take, I stepped outside, and I legitimately said to myself, "What the hell are you doing?"

See, I was trying to put myself back in my box the second I wasn't confident. I had put myself out there and got the role, but at that moment I wasn't confident and the voices in my head started with, "You don't need this, Aaron. Go home. You're a personal trainer, be fine with that." And then that little voice whispered real quietly and said, "No, stay." Everything ended up fine, and I'm so glad that I didn't listen to the loud voice. I listened to that little, tiny voice…that's the one.

Deantè: *So, the loud voice is the voice of doubt like the devil on your shoulder?*

Aaron: There it is right there, yes!

Deantè: *And the little voice is the reassurance and the angel on your shoulder?*

Aaron: Yes. The voice of confidence. They don't speak loudly, they speak quietly. But if you don't hear it, then you'll hear the loud voice saying, "Go home. You don't need this."

17.
MARCEL HORSLEY
Fear is Afraid of You

Co-owner of RevelHeir | Owner of Woods and Vines | 3 years in business

Marcel Horsley speaks about his company with such passion that I immediately wanted to buy one of his offerings. His journey through "losing" and "winning" is built on the sturdiest foundation imaginable: his parents. A lifetime of encouragement and being committed to his vision brought him to this place, and we're better for that. It is my privilege to present to you Marcel Horsley.

—D.Y.

Deantè: *Based on your life experiences, how important has failure been to your success?*

Marcel: It's been a big part of it. Not to sound too cliché, but without failure, you don't have success. People that work for me and have worked for me in the past, always hear me use the term "course correction" to mean getting from point A to point B. Within that is failure. I'll give you a perfect example: if you're on a plane going from Cleveland to Miami, all you know is that you went from Cleveland to Miami. You don't know everything that happened in between, which was the pilot going around a storm or elevating to a higher altitude...you only know that you went from point A to point B.

It's the same thing in business and in life. Course correction is key, and failure is a part of it. Early on, trying to get RevelHeir off the ground and started was tough. I came in as a partner. My business partner, a good friend of mine, acquired it in 2016, and it was stagnant for years. I have a business background and experience taking over businesses and building them from the ground up. Once I came in as a partner, things started moving in the right direction. Many trials and tribulations started early, but failure is definitely a part of success, and it's needed.

Deantè: *I would say that's extremely true for all of us. You said that you came in as a partner. So, what alerted you to the opportunity?*

Marcel: We have an umbrella company where we funnel all the business underneath. I've always been in the fashion industry, but I've also been into cigars and wines. The cigar and winery is my baby, and I feel as though this is what the culture needs. My business partner had other ideas and told me that I bring important things to the table that he lacks, so we're a tag team...strengths and weaknesses. He wanted to lay my eyes on something, and after discussing things, it was obvious that a partnership was necessary because the machine needed to be created.

You don't really have a machine coming out the gate; you must create it. We realized that I had the itch to get back into fashion from a distribution/mogul aspect as opposed to what he is really good at, which is the designing and styling aspect. We put our heads together and decided to make this thing win, and so far, we're winning.

Deantè: *Winning usually requires a lot of trial and error. On your journey so far, what were some of your biggest challenges to get you to where you are now?*

Marcel: The apparel. And COVID. Initially, we wanted to do a brick and mortar in Toledo to bring the world to Toledo. We realized that a lot of the folks here had not traveled outside of their city block. We travel a lot, and my business partner was very passionate about it. He wanted a brick-and-mortar store, and he had tunnel vision on this project. Then, the pandemic hit and one of the most beautiful things that happened was we didn't lose money. I had been an executive with Verizon for almost eleven years, but I left that position on February 28, 2020, and the pandemic hit a week later, so within that is a little bit of luck and a lot of faith in Christ, right?

Timing is everything, and if we would've pulled the trigger and closed on this building like we intended, we would've lost everything because at that point, the world had shut down. We weren't going to make a profit, and all of the money and resources would've been lost. 2020 was a blessing for me because the timing was so key for us that it allowed us to course correct and develop the idea of using an RV for the business. On the one hand, I had a business partner whose vision was brick and mortar, and on the other hand, there was me—the innovator, the outside-the-box thinker who stepped in and said, "Hey, let's revolutionize this and do something that no one's ever done, create our own lane and corner the market."

Selling him on the idea was a trial and tribulation in itself because where he only saw one way, here I was coming from left field to course correct and say, "This is what we can do." I took him to a couple RV lots and began explaining to him my vision of where the merchandise would go, which vendors we would use and so forth, and that made him finally see the vision.

Once we had that squared away, we began reaching out to vendors, Nike, Adidas, Asics—you name it. Then Nike threw us for a loop when they denied us because we didn't have a brick and mortar. Man! So, I had just closed my partner on the idea of going mobile, now Nike was telling us that they couldn't provide us with any products because we didn't have a physical address.

Adidas told us the same thing, but offered a back door solution to make it happen with them. All the other brands were on board, but because of the huge popularity of Nike and the Air Jordan line being the hottest in the game, we had to find a solution. We rented office space in downtown Toledo to establish an official address. Nothing had been said to us that we were required to *sell* from the address, just that we needed to have one. Using connections from my brother-in-law, we were able to get a workaround with Nike. We also partnered with a local designer who is killing the game right now with his unique shoes and his sales and we developed apparel for our mobile boutique that launched in August.

Deantè: *That is remarkable, man. Tony Robbins says that it's not about your resources; it's about your resourcefulness, and it's obvious that you guys are the embodiment of that.*

Marcel: Yes!

Deantè: *There is a perception that we must be confident to achieve difficult things. I personally believe that courage is more important* *than confidence. What experience comes to mind when you were afraid to try something because maybe you lacked self-belief?*

Marcel: This is probably the best question that you've presented so far, and I'll tell you why. I think it's important to have confidence, but I also think it's more important to be faithful and to have faith. With faith, you can almost destroy the fear, which gives you the courage. So yes, you need courage because fear will 100% cripple you, and it does that to every single person in this world. When you have that moment of "This is what I wanna do but I can't see the finish line in front of me, so I'm just gonna relax, but if I had all the answers, then I'd know I'll win and I'll do it. But if I don't have the answers and I can't see the success at the end, I'm more comfortable just staying where I'm at and doing this."

I gotta be honest with you. I've never gone for anything I didn't think I was going to get, and I learned this from my mom at an early age. She would say, "Jump out the window and know that the worst-case scenario is that you miss the trees and fall in the bushes." Because my mom and dad were present in my life, I could explore the world knowing I had them to be my safety net as if I were a tightrope walker. I knew if I fell, I would be okay because I would bounce back, which is the job of the safety net. So, I've had the ability all my life to jump out the window because I knew that playing Chess, I was gonna have a backup plan...a plan A or plan B.

I've never had the fear of "Not." My fear has always been "If I don't." If I didn't quit my job in February 2020, I wouldn't be in the position that I'm in today as an entrepreneur. When I was in corporate America, my fear was to not be able to retire at fifty, which was my goal, and I'm forty-two. The fear for me is not trying, and if I don't try, I'll be afraid of being stuck in the same position; I'm scared out of my mind of that because I'm like a bird. A bird only survives because it flies. I have to keep flying because if I don't, I fear I will fall victim to the societal predators such as mediocrity.

If I'm not better than I was yesterday, I worry that I let myself and my parents down. They always taught me, if I can be frank —"Jump out the fucking window!" Do you think a bird has to think twice before it takes flight for the very first time? No. It just knows it needs to get out of that tree or stay there and die.

Don't get me wrong, doubt does creep in often. Let's tie it back to February 28, 2020, because that's when I walked away from a six-figure income and, thankfully, my wife was very supportive of that. It was her idea for me to give my resignation letter, which I had typed in November 2019. I didn't know when I was gonna deliver it, but knew my time as a "worker" was coming to an end. No matter how far up the totem pole you go and become a boss, when you still gotta knock on someone else's door for time off...it's very humbling.

My dad passed unexpectedly in 2017, and in that first year after, I ran one of the busiest and most successful stores for Verizon. It was a well-oiled machine, so I asked my DM for time off to take my mom to Tennessee to be with her sisters and other family. I was told "No," even though I was fully staffed and would more than make up for the time off by working many other days including the entire weekend. At that point, I prayed to God: "If it's your will, I need to be out of retail," and I ended up being highly sought after for a better, more lucrative job with weekends and holidays off. I was running an entire territory, and it was such a blessing. Not long after, even though I got what I wanted the majority of the time, something in me realized I could do more.

I could do for my own business what I was already doing for that corporation. It just hit me, and my wife felt it was time for me to take the leap. When COVID first hit, things were still fine all the way up until 2021 when everything was lifted. Then, I started to miss my team and some of the things I did in the corporate world, and things that made me comfortable. A little fear and self-doubt crept in, and I thought, "Man, did I make the right decision?" Especially considering that I moved from a $115,000 annual income to everything that I have tied up in the business is my own personal money, not to mention other important financial commitments.

As you get closer to financial deadlines for things you prepared and your business hasn't fully blown up yet, it makes you miss knowing when that paycheck is coming. But then, you snap out of it. Self-doubt creeps in, but I realized that a burglar doesn't rob a house unless it's valuable. And the devil isn't gonna play with your mind unless he knows there's value there and what you're getting ready to do is God-worthy.

That's when you snap back to reality and say, "Oh! The devil's tugging at my heart and my mind, which means I'm doing something right, so I gotta shut the noise up and quiet that." But yeah, self-doubt does creep up sometimes.

Deantè: What advice would you give someone who is afraid to try because maybe they're afraid to fail?

Marcel: It's gonna sound cliche, but I would tell them to keep going. The failure is in *not* starting. Do you know how many great people in this world exist who we will never ever, ever in our lifetime get to see or enjoy their gifts and their abilities because they refused to try? And shame on them, and shame on whoever is reading or listening to this. Shame on you if you're that person because you owe it to me, the audience, the world, and yourself to use the gifts that God instilled in you.

If Michael Jordan decided to forget about playing basketball and instead did something else with his life once he was cut from his high school team, we would've never gotten to see one of the greatest athletes of all time. The economy would've missed out on more than a billion dollars in Air Jordan sales...think about that! If Anita Baker decided that she's only good at singing in the shower, my mom and dad wouldn't have met each other. Anita Baker was such a big part of what their relationship was; I still think of my mom and dad to this day when I hear her music.

If you don't try because you're afraid to fail, you are literally robbing us of legendary inventions, performances—you name it. You gotta do it because you owe it to yourself, and you owe it to the world. Peter Parker's uncle said, "With great power comes great responsibility," and he's right. Fear strengthens you, and my business partner will kill me because he owns the rights to this statement: "Fear is afraid of you." I live by that, and it's powerful because fear is the biggest bully in your life, and it will cripple you. As long as you allow fear to be the bully, you'll continue being the shy kid in the corner letting life pass you by and dictate where you should be instead of dictating your own successful moves.

Sometimes you gotta stand up to the bully and say, "I'm gonna do it," and if it doesn't work, it doesn't work. Go back to the drawing board and course correct that shit. But you gotta attempt and try. Otherwise, you'll become that flightless bird.

18.
BASHEER JONES:
Passion

Ward 7 Councilman of Cleveland, Ohio | Vice Chairman Health and Human Services Committee | 4 years in business

Basheer Jones is the ultimate social butterfly, which serves him well since he was the most interesting candidate in the race to become the next mayor of Cleveland. But I was most impressed with his immaculate perspective on overcoming pain and obstacles to ascend to a better place in life. He speaks with a distinctive eloquence which isn't just poetic; it inspires hope. It is my privilege to present to you Basheer Jones.

—D.Y.

Deantè: Based on your life experiences, how important has failure been to your success?

Basheer: It's everything. Many people have asked me, "Basheer man, aren't you afraid you're going to lose [his candidacy for Cleveland's next mayor]?" I said if I already have that mindset, I've already lost. No matter what happens, I won. No matter what happens, I had a chance to bring our issues to the forefront; I got a chance to talk about what's happening in my community. I got a chance to show the world that our community can produce intelligent Black men. So, no. I already won.

But falling is not failure. It is definitely a part of the journey. Failing is if you don't try.

It's necessary to get those scars on your knees and be told "No." I always tell my children that it's good to hear "No" sometimes, so they recognize that it doesn't stop anyone from moving forward. It's okay to hear "No," just don't let it stop you.

Deantè: *Yes. That's so powerful. Winning in life usually requires a lot of trial and error, lots of ups and downs. On your journey so far, what were some of your biggest challenges to get where you are now?*

Basheer: Just growing up in my community. Some of my biggest oppositions are people who look like me, come from where I come from, and family members. Also, just being Black in America sometimes creates mental health issues within us as a result of this existence. PTSD, you know. I said in one of my poems: "I got PTSD, and I never went overseas." I never fought overseas, but I grew up in a war zone. Where if you leave, you may not return—you know what I'm saying?

We live in war zone where family members and friends have been murdered. We deal with serious PTSD in our neighborhoods, so the emotional trauma that exists within us comes out in different forms within our relationships, whether marriages or interpersonal relationships or work relationships. It's a battle. Honestly, I'm going through it now just looking back at my life.

I grew up in the shelters of Cleveland. The shelters of New York. There's trauma that comes with those circumstances. And no matter how far we try to bury that pain, it shows up in different ways—in our experiences, how we express them, and how we express ourselves.

Deantè: *There is a perception that we must be confident to achieve difficult things. I believe courage is more important than confidence. What experiences come to mind when you were afraid to try something because you lacked self-belief?*

Basheer: I don't think you can have one without the other—you can't have courage without confidence, and you can't be confident without having courage. Especially in a society that tells you that you're not enough. All the time. It takes courage to say, "I *am* enough, and I don't care if no one else believes it or no one else says it. This is what it is. This is what I believe." I remember growing up as a young poet, hearing, "Ay man, poetry is for girls." I remember my teacher telling me that I talk too much and others saying discouraging things to me. As I grew up, I realized it wasn't a reflection of who I was; it was a reflection of who they were. So, I had to have the courage to keep on going.

At a young age, I didn't think of it as courage; I thought it was rejection. In their minds, it was me being arrogant. Some will mistake your courage or confidence for arrogance, and convince you that you're arrogant. They'll say someone else is confident, but continue to call you arrogant. So, we've dealt with that, but you just gotta keep on going, man. Keep pushing.

Deantè: *For sure. Okay, last question. What advice would you give to someone who is afraid to try because they are afraid to fail?*

Basheer: We all have a purpose in our lives. And if you don't fulfill your purpose, it will never be done, ever. So, I encourage each person to understand that whatever it is that God is guiding you to do. If *you* don't do it, it will never be done in the history of mankind the way that you have been guided to do it. That's my message—you are necessary and important, and if *you* don't believe it, nobody will.

19.
MARY JO MILLER:
Fearless

Owner, Bella Donna Salon & Spa, President of DPO | 36 years in business

Mary Jo Miller is one of the most impressive business executives I've ever met. I expected her to be soft spoken and reserved, but she is a tough-as-nails, no nonsense leader who handles challenges the way lions handle their prey. She is witty, funny and one of the most driven individuals there is. It is my privilege to present to you Mary Jo Miller.

—D.Y.

Deantè: Based on your life experiences, how important has failure been to your success?

Mary Jo: In business, I focus, and the only failure is *not* performing to my maximum ability. The pandemic was a great example of the ability to fail because we were closed for two and a half months. We had every disadvantage possible; the government shut us down, we had to adhere to mandates, which were good ones—to be able to stay safe. I put my nose to the grindstone and didn't give up. Failure is within you depending on how strong you are. You either have the stomach for business or you don't, and any kind of success is determined almost completely by one's self and their determination to succeed.

Your minor failures make you learn to never make the same mistake again because if you keep making that mistake, you obviously haven't learned anything from it, nor will you succeed at anything else. Keep learning from everything because the minute you stop learning, you'll never move forward.

My business is built on personal connection, and you should build your life on personal connections—who you meet, who you do things with, who you give back to, and your team. It's all interconnected, and success is all about the person who you are, and you are who you are by learning from the hurdles in your life. My biggest hurdle is being a female, and although that doesn't sound like much of a hurdle right now, when I started thirty-six years ago, I wouldn't have gotten a loan if I didn't have a female client who worked at Citizens Savings Bank.

Banks didn't want to give loans to females then, but she trusted me, and she knew what kind of worker I was, which is, "I don't have a shut off valve," That's another thing about success—I don't care if I have to stay up all night to get it done. Professionally, probably my biggest lesson was learning how to be a civically-minded, business-oriented female in this industry who stood up for herself. I also wanted to be involved in things even though people didn't want to see a woman who didn't act like a female, and it was a really difficult balance. Men treated me differently, and it was condescending when they would refer to me as "Honey." I was the first female to be on a board for several organizations.

Growing up with adversity shapes who you are, and you either get stronger, or you let it break you.

Deantè: Winning usually requires a lot of trial and error. On your journey so far, what were some of your biggest challenges to get you where you are now?

Mary Jo: You need to be financially solid to do the things I've done in business, and it takes guts and blind faith to think you can do it. When I added another building and did the necessary renovations, I took on a quarter-million dollars in debt. I have a lot of stupid faith sometimes, but I believed in what I was doing, and I felt comfortable. Right after expanding my building, the 2008 recession hit, and it was difficult. You can't control what you can't control. There are always setbacks, but that one was a doozy. The pandemic has been different in the fact that you can stay alive, or it can break you, and unfortunately, that happened a lot in my industry.

Some days, I would do five webinars, and I never put my head in the sand. You can't think, "Woe is me. What am I going to do now?" For me, it's always, "I will find out what I have to do" and not having a "shut off valve" helped because I just kept at it. I found out what I needed to do, and I looked ahead at what other states were doing, using California as my guideline because they were shut down longer than we were.

I've looked back at my life because of your questions, and I thought, "Who am I?" I'm just so used to who I've become that I never gave it much thought.

Deantè: *You're great at compartmentalizing things and you also don't dwell. Those are strong attributes to have.*

Mary Jo: I never thought of it like that, but I don't dwell on the past at all. Progressing with life, staying in the moment, and not living in the past has probably been a great thing for me.

Deantè: There is a perception that we must be confident to achieve difficult things, but I believe that courage is more important than confidence. What experiences come to mind when you were afraid to try something because maybe you lacked self-belief?

Mary Jo: I grew up with parents who wanted me to be a doctor, and I ended up not going to college, even though I was at the top of my class. I lacked the courage to go to college. When you're young, you sometimes lack courage for certain things, and mine was on a personal level. I was never afraid of business and the one and only time that I should've been afraid, I wasn't, even though it was the one big failure in my life.

Deantè: What happened?

Mary Jo: I had a restaurant that didn't work, and it was something I thought I could do. I had a couple of partners, which broke my own rule because not everybody has the drive. My husband told me that everybody isn't the same kind of worker and something else that sticks with me: "If they were like you, they would be you," and it's true. Not everybody has the desire to be in business or make significant sacrifices.

I've never been afraid of an adventure, and a lot of that is because of how I grew up. Early on, I felt as though I wasn't on the same par as others. Not in business, but in the community. Now, I don't feel intimidated talking to someone I don't know because of life experiences.

Deantè: *What advice would you give someone who is afraid to try something because they are afraid to fail?*

Mary Jo: Do something that you're good at and you love to do. Then, come up with a plan for how you're going to do it, and you can't be afraid. You'll never do anything if you're afraid, and being afraid is the worst thing you can do professionally. If you have done your homework and due diligence, you shouldn't be afraid. Fear of failure stops a lot of people, but if you have all the pieces together, a good plan, and the drive to do it, you shouldn't be afraid.

You can't blindly go into something and say it's going to work because that's when you need to be afraid. Not knowing what you're doing before jumping in is scary, and many people do that. Having a passion is great, but without a plan and the willingness to start small, which wasn't easy for me, you will fail.

If you have a plan, a passion, and you love what you're doing, it's hard to fail.

20.
ALLISON OCCKIAL: YOU CAN'T WIN UNLESS YOU PLAY

CEO, Finesse Fitness | Wellness Coach | Personal Trainer | Nutritionist | 9 years in business

Allison Occkial has the impenetrable discipline of the rising of the morning sun. Her journey to greatness is jaw dropping in the way it served her large helpings of adversity—only for her to turn that trash into treasure. As a wellness coach, her acumen and proficiency is second to none, largely because she is her own best "student." It is my privilege to present to you Allison Occkial.

—D.Y.

Deantè: Based on your life experiences, how important has failure been to your success?

Allison: It has played a major role because when you "fail," it's a chance to pause and reassess; it's only a failure if you stop trying or give up. Instead of using the word "failure," it's more of a challenge in the whole journey. So, "failing" has allowed me to pause, reassess, pivot, and change my direction without losing sight of the drive or passion. You're still moving forward, but failure can shift you in different directions. It's definitely helped me to increase motivation, be more humble, lower the ego that plays into our lives, and improve my overall growth as a person, personal development, and learning through life.

Deantè: Whenever I say the word "failure," I'm referring to society's perception of failure. I agree with you that failure is not actually failure; it's a life experience or life lesson that can also provide feedback from the situation. So, I think you're spot on with that.

Allison: I like that word, and I was trying to find a substitution for "failure," but it is basically feedback from what you are doing or not doing. Feedback is a much more neutral word. Failure is obviously negative.

Deantè: Yes. It's amazing that society views failure as failure. So, winning usually requires a lot of trial and error. On your journey so far, what were some of your biggest challenges to get you where you are now?

Allison: About ten years ago, several major things happened in my life. My dad passed away suddenly, and I was in a long-term romantic relationship that was emotionally and mentally toxic and not supportive. Going through that, I realized the importance of challenges and relationships with the people in my life. I also realized life is not guaranteed, and the importance of living our lives and not settling.

Going after things you want and what truly matters will be different for each person, but that kind of woke me up. When you're 24, you're still figuring out who you are and what you want in life, and I realized I needed to do stuff for myself and push myself. I lost my dad in 2011, and on New Year's Day 2012, I moved out of the house that I was living in with my long-term boyfriend because I felt that wasn't for me anymore. It was scary when I ripped off that Band-Aid. I also started doing fitness competitions because I had always wanted to, but was scared to at first, but finally pushed myself to do it. I also met my husband that year, so looking back, I needed that low point in my life in 2011 to realize I'm better and I can have more and be more for other people, which has led me to where I am today.

After losing my dad, I wanted to help others avoid the same situation I experienced, whether for them or so they didn't have to see a family member suffering and lose them suddenly. I wanted to help others improve their health; I didn't know what I know now that could've helped my dad, and I want to share that with others, which started the trajectory of where I am now.

Throughout my mid-20s, I was dealing with some hormonal imbalances and other health struggles. I had a new job, but I also hit a ceiling at that job. So, there were personal issues and career issues, and I decided to use those experiences to not settle and keep moving forward. I was my own advocate, whether personally or in my career, standing up for myself knowing I could be better, do more, and be the best version of myself. I've had to apply the lessons I first experienced ten years ago to different chapters of my life.

Deantè*: You went through a lot of trials and tribulations. Losing your dad so suddenly and having a toxic relationship are both debilitating. It seems everything you've achieved thus far has happened because of those things, not in spite of them. It's a lesson to all of us that we need to go through the rotten times because in some way, shape or form, they mold us into who we're supposed to be.*

Allison: Yes, and I don't regret that relationship, but I obviously miss my dad. Of course, I didn't want that to happen. But it is what it is, so I decided to learn from it and figure out what I could do for myself personally and help others from it.

Deantè: *All of us are better off because of it. You were sharpening your axe and didn't realize it. Now, what experience comes to mind when you were afraid to try something because you lacked self-belief? I know many of us believe that we have to have confidence, but I think courage is more important than confidence.*

Allison: I love that question. I agree that courage is much more important than confidence. I was afraid to turn my business into a full-time wellness practice because I had been doing it part-time while attending school for other certifications. Plus, I'd hit a ceiling with the job I had at the time, still in the health field full-time and doing personal training part-time. I decided that I couldn't do both. There was no more growth for me at my job, although I enjoyed it. I figured that in five years, I would still be doing the same thing. The scary and courageous thing to do was to turn my business into a full practice of health coaching and nutrition, utilizing what I had just learned in school, and help more people in a broader scheme. But it was 100% on me, so there was no boss or assistant I could go to, which was scary yet one of the best things I've ever done for myself personally and professionally.

Deantè: *You weren't entirely sold that you could do it, were you intimidated at all?*

Allison: Yes! Because there's no guarantees. I could've started it and had no clients. Then there's the business aspect of it—actually doing the coaching, programming, backend, marketing, accounting, and billing. But I know that you can't win unless you play. You have to take that risk so I asked myself, given my situation, if I stayed where I was at, what would the outcome be? If I decided to take my business full-time, what could happen? I could fail, or it could be the best thing of my life. I didn't know unless I tried and put myself out there.

Deantè: It's great to know that you had doubts because you seem so self-assured now, and when we see the journey of great people, and I put you in that category, it actually helps the rest of us believe that we can do things. We tend to put great people on pedestals, like "Oh they were flawless and no troubles or struggles during their journey." But you saying what you just said actually makes people say, "Wow, if she had doubts, then it's okay for me to have doubts. The only difference is she overcame them and didn't let them stop her." So, that's powerful.

Allison: Yep.

Deantè: What advice would you give someone who is afraid to try because they are afraid to fail?

Allison: I have eight bullet points. Number one, retrain and constantly prepare your mind. You must have at least 1% belief in yourself that you can do it. This will drive your behavior and your ultimate results, knowing that doubts and fear are all normal and valid emotions. Our physiology goes towards comfort, and resists any change or discomfort.

But you have to choose your "uncomfortable:" choosing to stay where you are now, which is uncomfortable if you're not happy, or choosing the discomfort of trying something new and possibly failing. Remember, there is a possibility you will succeed—you need to decide.

Number two, have a specific plan because if you just think you're going to be successful and don't push the gas pedal to go somewhere, it's a moot point. You're not going to do anything or be successful.

Number three, recruit, support and accountability. You must create an environment that will be successful, and that entails asking friends and family, business mentorship, or whatever else you need. Also, find a spiritual point of view and, personally, I use God's strength to drive me and to understand that I can't do everything on my own, and I am not expected to.

We must learn how to be humble and to ask for help and support when we need it. Successful people don't get to where they want to be by being closed minded and thinking they can do it all on their own. You must be humble enough to say, "I'm okay at this, but I suck at that, but I wanna get better at it." Ask the right questions: "What do I need to do?" and "How can I improve?" while being willing to learn.

Number four, daily and weekly practices on checking in with yourself through journaling and affirmations. Have different mantras and consistency for when doubts come in. You're still going back to Number one, which is retraining your mind.

Number five, celebrate your wins and focus on the positives. That's part of this book; how we can shift from negative to positive, or at least a more neutral standpoint. Even a one-degree difference makes a huge difference in our results. If you decide to walk for one more minute today, or that you're going to bed one minute earlier or leaving one less bite on your plate—what if you did those things every day? That adds up. We don't think about it in the long-term, but those small wins make a big difference.

Make sure that you're being humble, while still being your best cheerleader. Be humble enough to change your direction, but not your drive and your passion. What you want to achieve, which is your ultimate "why," would still be there, but you might have to do things a little differently to get there.

Lastly, if you feel like you're doubting yourself—don't have a "What if?" That means that if you don't do X, what could happen? Don't allow yourself to be in that spot. Maintain the "You can't win if you don't play" concept. Don't make "not knowing how it would've turned out" be okay if you fail to try something. If you think you might regret not trying later, that means you should go for it when you can. Whatever you are resisting is usually what you need to do the most.

Deantè: *That is the most spot-on advice. Do you ever have anything that you resist that's troubling for you even now, but you somehow fight through it?*

Allison: Yes. In different aspects of my life, for sure.

Deantè: *That's amazing because you seem like Wonder Woman.*

Allison: Make sure you know the running dialogue in your head because that will ultimately create your success. You could easily let the negatives fester, and I'll give you an example: workouts. Many people struggle with doing them and find a million reasons not to exercise. They'll even be in the middle of a workout and want to quit and think, "If I quit the workout early, will that bring me closer to my goal or farther away?"

I also have different mantras and affirmations like, "Choose your uncomfortable," "Embrace the suck," and "Actions over words." You can be mentally there, but if your behavior doesn't match your words, you won't get the results you want. You can say, "I wanna lose ten pounds" or "I wanna get healthier," but if you don't follow through with the workout, it's not going to happen.

I tell myself these things all day long, and it's to the point where I don't really even think about it anymore because it's so natural. Acknowledge when those doubts, fears, and insecurities creep in, and you tell yourself "No, I'm better than that. I know this is tempting and I know this is what I want to do naturally, but I'm choosing the alternate route."

21.
MATTHEW PARKS: Preaching is Easy. Practicing is Hard

Husband | Father | Work in Progress | 12 years in business

Matthew Parks told me to list him as a "work in progress" for his chapter. He is so unimpressed with himself that his luminous achievements in business deserve nary a mention—in his opinion. Therein lies his exceptionalism; he is a man on a mission to be better for others, build them up and do it while setting the example with his own attempts at self-mastery. It is my privilege to present to you Matthew Parks.

—D.Y.

Deantè: Based on your life experiences, how important has failure been to your success?

Matt: Not as important as successful people's failures have been to my success. I can learn from my own mistakes, or I can learn from other people's mistakes. I figured, "Why would I go through that pain if someone else already has, and extract the lesson from their loss?" Why wouldn't I just take that and avoid going down that same path? So, I've really tried to pay attention to people I admire, their dos and don'ts, and shortcut the process. If you burn your hand on a stove, and you showed me, "Hey, look. This is what happened when I touched this thing," I'm never touching it again.

If I respect you and what you've done, I'm going to take your word for it and not touch the stove. I've learned from my own failures for sure, and I think you have to, but you gotta try to learn from the failures of successful people. Failing doesn't make you a failure, quitting does. But failing in itself doesn't make you a failure. Getting advice from failures (quitters) is not good advice.

A person who quits, or fails, normally blames others. When a winner fails, they look in the mirror, figure out what they did wrong, and make adjustments. When a loser fails, they take very little, if any, ownership, and looks to place the blame somewhere else. So, it's hard to get lessons from a quitter because it was never their fault.

Deantè: *That's really a good perspective. A lot of times, you can't tell people things because they don't want to listen. What gave you the wherewithal and desire to listen to successful people when they would tell you something? We all believe we are know-it-alls, and that usually starts in our teen years.*

Matt: I didn't think I was a know-it-all, so maybe that's the difference. I think I was the opposite of a know-it-all because I felt like I didn't know shit and I needed to know more. So, on this quest to learn, I discovered that the more you learn, the more you realize how much you don't know, so that made me want to continue learning. It amplified that desire, so, to me, it was not really a challenge, and I didn't have to fight my ego at all. I already lacked confidence, and others say that I had humility, but I probably lacked confidence because I didn't feel like I knew a whole lot.

So, I had to seek it. I'm always amazed at people who think they know so much about something that they've never experienced. I find it funny when people say, "Well, I woulda done this..." So, why aren't you doing that? Like a Monday morning quarterback—it's very easy to do that when you're not in the game dodging a linebacker, ya know what I mean?

Deantè: *Well, it sounds like you have incredible self-awareness, which is one of the biggest assets that anyone can have, so I admire that. Now, winning usually requires a lot of trial and error. On your own personal journey so far, what were some of your biggest challenges to get to where you are?*

Matt: Probably fighting the self-doubt that I think everybody has when trying something new. I try to turn the fear of the unknown into the excitement of the unknown. I think that other people's opinions, as much as we want to act like they don't matter, do matter to most of us. And so the challenge is, "What are other people gonna think about me if I do this or if I say that or if I try this career path or if I quit this career or if I get married again or get divorced again...whatever adjustments or life changes or directions or passions you wanna pursue, there's always this fear maybe, or worry about what are they gonna think of me?" And most of the time, people aren't looking at you, and it's all in your head.

Some of that has been a challenge for me, as well as normal self-doubt. For instance, when I came to American Income, I was already in a good career and making good money from the world's view. People would look at me like, "Hey, you're successful. Why would you leave a job that's got certainty to go over here where there's more unknown?" That's another challenge, I think. As you get into things, the biggest challenge is not thinking long-term. We get caught up in what's happening right now, and we don't remember that today is just one day of many days. You can start convincing yourself that one bad day means you made a bad decision, but that's not always the case. So, you need to have a bigger vision and factor in setbacks, tough days, and rough days—not only in business.

If you're an athlete who's training for the Olympics, you have to have the big picture in your mind as you're swimming every single day. All day, you're either eating or swimming, and once you're done swimming, you have to start eating. I remember reading that Michael Phelps had to consume 17,000 calories a day just during his practice, and how hard is that to do? That's tough because when he wasn't eating, he was in the pool. When he wasn't in the pool, he had to eat to get the energy to keep going back in the pool, and that's a four-year commitment. I'm not just talking about him; I'm talking about anyone who's done something super special like that. They commit to the big picture and break it down like, "Alright, I just gotta get through today." Because if he starts telling himself, "Holy shit, I gotta do this for four years; eat, swim, eat, swim, sleep, eat, swim," he'll become overwhelmed. "Instead, he might have to say, "Alright, it's July 21st, 2021. My goal today is to get my calories in, get my swims in, and do it the right way." You gotta bring it into one day, and you can't quit on the whole goal because you have a bad day. Just say, "Hey, I'm gonna show back up tomorrow." So, have an overall picture that gives you the power to push through tough days, and try to win each day one at a time. Why worry about tomorrow?

A guy named James Lawrence has a Netflix documentary called *Iron Cowboy*. This dude is just a massive, massive badass. He ran fifty Iron Mans—in fifty days, in fifty states. Look him up and watch his documentary. You will be like, "Oh my Lord." Then he did one hundred in a row in one hundred days, but he didn't go to different states.

In the documentary, he talked about how he literally just had to get through one step at a time; an Iron Man consists of swimming, running, and biking. Fifty in a row, every day in a different state! So, he had to travel, recover, deal with logistics and weather, while taking care of his body and his family.

He kept saying that if he started thinking about "Man, I got thirty-five more of these," there's no way he would've completed it. He had to zero in on the next step. He wouldn't even refer to it by the day; he would break it down by saying, "Next step, next step. I got one mile to go." So, there's something about the mind that allows people to have a bigger purpose to push through the temporary discomforts that will come no matter where you're at or what you do.

Deantè*: Wow. Would you say that mentality applies to even your personal life? You're a father and a husband now, and there's always challenges with those things, too.*

Matt: Without a doubt. If my daughter's not listening to me, I'm like, "I want her to listen! I want her to listen because I want her to be a good human when she gets out into the world." But I have to zero it down to a specific situation and be patient. I have to teach her the lessons and I can't think, "Oh she's not listening. She's gonna be a bad human." Sometimes my mind will go there, like "Man, if she doesn't start listening, she's gonna be one of those kids in school who gets suspended." I can't go down that path and think, "Oh, I gotta fix it!" Really, I need to be patient and let her make some mistakes.

I just have to help her, love her, and know how to correct her behavior today. It's always a battle, and sometimes you wonder, "Am I doing this right? Am I being too hard? Am I being too easy? Am I being too patient? Am I not being patient enough? Am I letting her get away with too much? Am I being too strict? She's three and a half…" There's no recipe on this, and a lot of it is trial and error. I talk to other parents who at least appear to have done a decent job with their kids. It's a tough one, man. I've seen great parents do the best they can, and the kids still do what they want. That's a real tough one because you're banking on the behavior of another person. Think about how hard it is to control your own behavior. Now we're trying to do that to somebody else whose brain isn't fully developed yet. We're really grasping at straws when we put too much faith in that.

Deantè: *We definitely have to get lucky on how they turn out no matter how we raise them.*

Matt: I'm learning that more and more.

Deantè: *There is a perception that we have to be confident to achieve difficult things. I believe that courage is more important than confidence. What experience comes to mind when maybe you were afraid to try something because you lacked self-belief?*

Matt: I think that confidence is earned through courage. How are you confident if you don't ever act courageous? What would make someone confident if they're always backing out the moment they smell a little uncertainty? I think you earn your way to confidence by demonstrating courage, doing things you are not sure about, and taking chances—which don't need to be irresponsible, you can take calculated risks.

You have to show yourself that you're willing to try. I was nervous to make a career jump at twenty-seven years old when I was already in a good situation. I was not confident when I started, but I was excited. I turned the fear into excitement; it's the same feeling except one's expecting a bad outcome and one's expecting a good outcome. The only difference between fear and excitement is the anticipation that something is going to happen.

Fear is worry that something bad will happen. Excitement is hope that something amazing will happen. They're both unknown, and both elicit the same chemical feeling inside you. However, one has a terrible outcome, and one has a great outcome.

I had to shift my mind to focus on, "This isn't fear; this is excitement because it's gonna end up being great. Well, what if it's not? Well, what if it is?" Get your repetitions to a place where you feel like you've earned confidence, too. You probably won't be good at anything you do for the first time. So, if you go in understanding that and you're willing to fail, learn, and grow and you don't look at the failure as a final thing, but just as an adjustment period, then you're gonna be okay.

People are afraid to fail all the time. It's rare that you get anywhere if you're not willing to fail temporarily. You didn't learn how to walk by giving up every time you fell. You didn't learn how to write by walking away every time you're about to put something on paper. You got better at it by "doing." Repetition creates a skill over time. If I was a basketball player and wanted to dribble with my left hand, I gotta do it. I can't just think about it; I have to dribble the ball. I may bounce it off my knee or my foot, and the ball will likely be stolen from me a few times.

But if I do it every day, I'll suck a little less at it in a week from now than I do today. In two weeks, I'll suck a little less than that, and in a month, hell, I might not even suck anymore. I may just be decent. And in another month, I may not be just decent, I may be okay. And I can go from "okay" to, you know what? I got some handles with my left now. And before you know it, I can go to the hoop with my left and finish. Now I'm a threat because I can go left, and I can go right. But...will you, will I, and will someone go through the process of bouncing it off their knee and not seeing that immediate result and go through that discomfort and go through those failings—without stopping?

That's what we said at the beginning; failing is fine. Failure is when you quit.

Deantè: That's a great distinction. I never thought of it that way. It reminds me of a time when you said, "I'm never down. I'm either up or I'm getting up." That's something that sticks with me.

Matt: John Maxwell said that; I just stole it.

Deantè: It doesn't matter, you're a vessel.

Matt: All of this stuff is stolen by the way. I'm not coming up with any of this on my own. I've read, studied, and learned... again, studying the successful people. They talk about, "Hey listen, I was willing to fail. I looked at my fear, and thought, why am I scared? I should be excited. This is an unknown, it could turn out great." And the other thing is having a perspective on your life. There's an old country song, and I can't remember who sings it, about a guy talking about living like he was dying.

He talks about going skydiving and doing all this stuff...our days are always numbered, no matter what. I'm not saying to start skydiving. I'm just saying that you can do some things that you're a little uncertain of, and it'll probably make you feel *more* alive. If you found out you had less than a year to live, you would absolutely be more eager to try things that you might not do now because you think you have a lease on life.

That perspective, that today's a blessing, live it up...now people take that to the extreme, right? "Man, live it up, you only live once," or "YOLO, you only live once, so let's party it away…" You can take anything and make it an extreme where it can be dangerous for you. You gotta temper all that.

Deantè: I think those guiding principles helped to minimize your self-doubt. You're reframing things.

Matt: Yes, it's perspective. Think about a picture that when you look at it, it's a scary old lady. But if you look at it a different way, it's a beautiful woman.

Deantè: What advice would you give someone who is afraid to try something because they are afraid that they might fail?

Matt: I would say being afraid to fail is normal, being afraid to fail is fine, but be willing to anyway. There's more regret in the "not doing," than there is in the "doing and failing" almost every time. Most people don't look back and regret the things they did. From what I've seen, they regret the things they wanted to do and never freakin' sacked up and did. So, I feel like it's just a heavier weight to carry because if you do it and you fail, you can let go of that and keep moving. If you learn from it, you should become stronger and move forward.

But if you keep punking out, then regret just builds because it hasn't left you. You're like, "I really wanna try it, but I'm too scared." That just adds weight to you, and you try to climb up in life, and it's like adding a weighted backpack that gets heavier and heavier and heavier. The longer you go, the heavier it gets, so you might as well just do it already. Shed that weight, take your lesson—it could be a loss, it could be a lesson, it could be a win that you double down on. But not doing it is guaranteed extra weight. You don't regret not doing most things, unless we're talking about something that's really asinine and stupid, uncalculated and foolish. But we're not normally talking about that.

This is not, "should I try Heroin?" No. I'm talking about calculated real stuff that can push you forward in life and gives you a more exhilarating feeling that's not crazy, life-threatening, or insane.

22.
ERIC SEAN:
FROM THE FLAMES WE RISE

Life Purpose Coach | Author | Motivational Speaker | Personal Trainer | 30 years in business

Eric Sean endured mental and psychological pain during his childhood so unimaginable that he could've become a serial killer and it would've been understandable. Instead, he used that horror to build himself into an extraordinary man—one who excels as an entrepreneur and transforms people into better versions of themselves. It's his signature gift to a world that failed to destroy him. It is my privilege to present to you Eric Sean.

—D.Y.

Deantè: *Based on your life experiences, how important has failure been to your success?*

Eric: In hindsight, failure has been probably one of the most crucial components of success. Most of my life, I've viewed myself as a failure. Because of that, everything I did or thought was filtered through the mind of a failure, so I failed continuously. And it was through consistently failing that I was forced to find out who I was.

Deantè: *You're saying that you had self-esteem issues?*

Eric: I had extreme self-esteem issues, and they follow me still to this day. I was born from a sixteen-year-old mother who was a prostitute, drug addict, and was very lost. She was also incarcerated at the time. From the moment I was born, within five days, I was in foster care. My mindset from a very early age was that if your mother doesn't want you, there's something wrong with you. And in my mind, all I knew was I couldn't perceive the reality that she was going through her own situations; in my mind, she didn't want me.

From five days old, I was in foster care. I was physically, emotionally, sexually, and mentally abused. I remember in one foster home, I had to be around six years old because I went to my second foster home when I was seven. Back then, parents would beat you--it was punishment, and they would pick up the closest thing to whoop you with. By age six, I was so tired of it that I actually reached back to block whatever it was that she was hitting me with, and it happened to be a board with a nail in it. My finger still has the mark from it.

So, that's the type of abuse that I endured. In my second foster home, my foster mom hated being able to hear me scream from a whooping, and we would have to go out to the yard and find the right switch—old-school stuff. So, I would have to go out, find the switch, and she would have me lay down on my back, put a pillow over my head and sit on the pillow so she didn't have to hear me scream. When she felt like I had a good enough whooping, I would have to sit in the hot tub afterwards.

With my young mind, there was only one way that I could perceive all of it. I was going through *this* life because I was nothing and was destined to be a failure. When I was nine years old, I was adopted by a single, white homosexual man, and he was the best thing to ever happen to me, but I saw it all in hindsight. I couldn't see it then. At that point in my mind, my whole race knew I was no good and gave up on me. So, when this white man adopted me, I saw all kinds of crazy stuff. I went from the ghetto to an all-white neighborhood, to an all-white Catholic school. So, the self-hate and the disrespect that I had for myself and the lack of value that I felt only got worse because now I looked nothing like anyone else at school or in my neighborhood. So all of that feeling like a failure, and I elaborate on this because I think when most people fail, they feel like a failure, which stops them from trying the next thing.

Most of my adolescence and into adulthood I felt like a failure. By the time I was fourteen, I had been in and out of drug treatment centers three different times because I felt worthless, and I felt like a failure, and I felt that my life was destined to fail. Anything I touch because of my mindset, and I'm really big on mindset, I did nothing but create situations in which I would fail. Because of how the mind works, whatever you send out, you're going to attract like. So, since I sent out a persona of being a failure, all I got was more failure.

My life got to the point where I went a year and a half bouncing from couch to couch and finally got to the point that I ate out of a garbage can because I was so hungry. All of that brought me to a point when I had a bad drug and alcohol problem, where I had been up for three days doing cocaine. I was sitting in my living room, and by the way, I'm a big 2Pac fan, listening to one of his songs over and over. Then a moment came while listening to this song when I didn't want to kill myself, but I knew I couldn't go on living the way that I was living.

So, I had to decide to either do something to change my life or I was gonna cease to exist. I think that's what most people go through. I went through it on a large scale, but even on an individual scale, I think people go through a place where they face failure and they have to decide that it's either a learning experience and they pull strength from that situation, and they try it again, or they need to try a different approach. The power behind failing is that it forces you to try a different approach. Through all these experiences of feeling like a failure, I got to that moment of clarity where I knew in my logical mind, I couldn't come up with a rationalization. I couldn't justify it, and I knew that I did not have the answer.

So, I was forced to try a different approach. Failure ultimately brought me to a place where I had learned enough, taken the lessons, and knew there had to be more. There had to be another "try." I was sick of being down, and in order to stand up, I had to try a different way.

Deantè: *Wow. That's explosive, man. Do you think when listening to 2Pac something in his lyrics or the passion in his voice made that your turning point, or was it all the other things going on in your life at the time?*

Eric: I think it was a combination of both. The name of the song was "Better Dayz," and I've always been really big on lyrics. I can't tell you what the lyrics were, but I know they were in reference to wanting more out of life and being able to see a bigger vision. That's what I was faced with at that moment. And then I met a Buddhist Sensei, who helped me change my life. Failure is like a crossroads. When you come to a point where you feel like you've failed, you either can give up or use it to motivate and catapult you into something different.

I think the energy behind making a decision to try something different is like the old saying, "When the student is ready, the teacher will appear." When we fail and we try something different, the resources for that journey show up, which is what happened to me. This guy had a completely different philosophy, and he helped me believe there was more in life, and I was only a failure if I decided I was a failure. Isn't that what goes on in the mind of anyone when they fail? You have to determine if you're a failure or if your approach failed. If you can say, "This approach failed, and there's another way," you'll see that there's another way and another option.

He helped me realize that I could be successful, I deserved to be like everybody else and accomplish anything, opening the door for me to be in a position where I wanted to learn more. And it's been a growing experience ever since.

Deantè: Because of their life experiences, people will often stay in a debilitating mental space. When you think about all the things you went through, it's amazing that this Buddhist could get you out of that place and on the right track, where you stayed. What would you attribute that to?

Eric: Internally, I never lost hope. I always knew there was something more, but because of my mindset, I couldn't figure out what it was. I had to lose faith in my mindset to be open to something different. Up until that point, my mindset was the only thing I knew. I ran into the Buddhist at the point where I knew my mindset didn't work, and he offered an alternative. Drugs and alcohol were always great medicine for me, and they helped me cope. All of my defenses and the guardedness that I possessed helped me to cope, and was something I needed.

The Buddhist gave me an equal or greater medicine by helping me to realize that not only was I my problem, but I could also be my solution.

Deantè: *Winning usually requires a lot of trial and error. On your journey so far, what were some of your biggest challenges to get you to where you are now?*

Eric: I always believed that money was hard to come by. And because of that, I didn't think it could come to me easily because that wasn't my agreement. So, I always worked against myself. I've been in the fitness industry for thirty years, but if I'm being honest with you, eighteen of those years weren't very profitable. The only thing that kept me in it was my passion; there wasn't any money. And there was no money because I didn't believe I could earn money (because it was hard to come by). I always charged way too little, because you gotta work your ass off to make money. So, I did way, way, way more work than I had to and charged absolutely nothing because that was my agreement.

I would open a gym, and the gym would ultimately fail because I was working too hard and not making enough money. So, I would try to do things differently, and it would be a little bit more profitable. Ultimately, it wasn't profitable until I realized and changed that agreement that money comes to me with ease from multiple sources. Once I adopted that mentality, the money just came.

I've had gyms and I've been evicted from buildings because I wasn't able to pay my bills. But, I had so much belief in what it was I was trying to do, I always figured out a way to keep it going. Then, the situation would happen again. I might have one or two good years, but because of that belief, it would fail again. In terms of relationships, I grew up without a mom, and then my first foster mom died, so I had to go to a second foster home. In my mind, two of my moms had left me, so I absolutely didn't deserve to have a working relationship with women, and women would always leave.

So, I sabotaged every relationship that I had. In my mind, they were gonna leave anyway because of the agreement I had. Until I changed that agreement, I couldn't have a healthy relationship because I would make sure I ruined the relationship before they left me. Again, it's the mentality. I failed over and over and over again in relationships until I was able to take a good look at my thought process and figure out how to correct it.

That's why I'm so adamant about mindset because it's all about mindset. Everything we do is about mindset. You can take two people and put them in the exact same failure situation, and they'll react completely differently. The person who's successful, number one, has always made a decision that, whatever it takes, this is gonna happen. The other person has made a wish list of "I would like for this business to be successful," but when it starts failing, any obstacle will get in their way.

The person who decided they will be successful will always be successful. Once you make a decision, it *has* to come true. Once you make a true decision that something will happen, it must come true because you'll figure out a way for it to happen. If you fail fifty times, if you've made a decision that it's gonna work, it's gonna work.

Deantè: *How do you get through the tough times? Is it just the passion? It has to be something that you're passionate about, like you said about what kept you going during those thirty years where eighteen were not profitable. It was because you had a passion for what you were doing. Is that the key to staying locked in when times get rough?*

Eric: Yes. It's a belief. William James, an old philosopher, said, "Believe and your belief will create the facts." If you believe in something strongly enough, you'll make it happen. There's a saying, "I was so focused on the objective that the obstacles had to fall to the wayside." If you're so focused on what you want to create or do, everything else is just obstacles, and those come and go. But you have an unwavering belief and an unwavering decision that this will happen. It comes down to believing that your belief combined with your decision will ultimately create an action that will make it come true.

Deantè: *It sounds like you're talking about a self-fulfilling prophecy.*

Eric: A thousand percent. If you make a decision that it is, it is. If you make a decision that it isn't, ultimately, you're gonna sabotage yourself or do something and it won't be.

Deantè: *There is a perception that we have to be confident to achieve difficult things. I believe that courage is more important than confidence. What experience comes to mind where you were afraid to try something because maybe you didn't think you could do it?*

Eric: I agree with you on that a thousand percent, but I think it's a combination. Confidence is something you can muster up in your mind. You can be very confident about something, but that confidence is a theory, and it doesn't become fact until you can muster up enough courage to actually do it. You can have a wonderful conversation with yourself and become very confident and tell yourself, "I'm about to go do this," but when it comes down to it and you have to do it, that's where that courage steps in.

I've been confident about so many things. Last year, I got my pro card in bodybuilding, and I worked with two different coaches. I couldn't stick to the meal plan the first coach gave me. In my mind, I could say that I was gonna win all day because I was confident that I would. But my actions didn't show it, and I didn't have the courage to give up certain things. I always knew that I would win, but it wasn't until I had the courage to do something different and to give up the stuff preventing me from winning that I wanted that it actually came true.

So, you need to have confidence, but I agree that what's even more important in turning that theory into a fact is breaking through what I call the "Terror Barrier." There's a barrier of fear and no matter how confident you are, you won't be able to achieve what it is you want to achieve until you bust through that barrier and get to the other side. That terror barrier is so thick sometimes, that even someone with the greatest theory won't be able to do it.

Deantè: *It's shocking to hear that you had a problem giving up food, and it sounds like something that was relatively recent.*

Eric: Oh yeah. That was about a year ago.

Deantè: *That's amazing. You're built like the 1985 version of Arnold Schwarzenegger, and since you have accomplished so much, it obviously shows that you have great will. But in spite of all that, you still have something challenging to do, and that's great for the rest of us. People like you can seem out of reach for the rest of us, but you still have those moments where you fall short. It's more important to hear these things than to hear about your successes because this makes us feel like we can do it.*

Eric: Anybody at any level, if they're transparent, will tell you that they always face a little bit of nervousness and fear. You never really lose the fear; you just gain a precedent in your mind that lets you know you can get through the fear or challenge. But you still have to get through it every single time. It becomes easier, but there's still a little bit of terror.

I'll give you an example. I've had the privilege to have some phone conversations and one-on-ones with Les Brown. And Les will be the first one to tell you that although he knows he'll get on stage and do an amazing job, there's still a level of nervousness. He will also tell you that if you're doing anything and there's no nervousness, you shouldn't be doing it. Nobody is above anything; some of us have more experience, but everybody deals with the exact same thing.

If you ever get to the point in life where there is no struggle, that means that there's nothing more to learn. And when there's nothing more to learn, there's no reason for you to be here anymore. No matter how much work you've done, nobody becomes God. We all still deal with the same human things and that's why I always say to anybody, "I'm not above you and I never wanna be above you. I wanna be right beside you because this is a life journey that we're all taking together. Anything I've dealt with and been able to find a solution to, I wanna share it with you. The only way I can really share it with you is by walking with you. I never wanna be an authority on anything because there's always stuff to learn."

Deantè: What advice would you give someone who is afraid to try because maybe they are afraid to fail?

Eric: I would say that the person who risks nothing, gains nothing, learns nothing and, therefore, has nothing. Anything in life of any value that's worth having involves risk and hard work. There are no shortcuts to anywhere worth going, so you have to take a risk. Without risk, there's no payoff. Turning that theory of what you want into a reality happens when you walk through the terror barrier. And once you go through it one time, it'll still be there, but it'll be so much easier the next time.

23.
JAMES SURACE:
WALKING IN POWER

Senior Partner and Founder of Surace-Smith and Partners Insurance Group | Entrepreneur | Philanthropist | Ordained Christian Minister | Board Member of United in Christ International, HarvestNet Ministries and Hydrating Humanity | Founder and CEO of ASAP America | 39 years in business

James Surace is a highly regarded business magnate, a scintillating philanthropist, and a man of God. But his true legacy lies in his expansive mentorship of scores of high achievers in business and in his youth programs. Behind that long tenured greatness is Nancy Surace, married to James for 42 years, and who serves as his indispensable partner. It is my privilege to present to you James Surace.

—D.Y.

Deantè: Based on your life experiences, how important has failure been to your success?

James: It's been everything. Failure brings you to a place in the valley, and for me, it happened in 1990. When I started with the company, I had a meteoric career. Everything was going great; I was tops in sales in the country and was promoted to run the state of Ohio, all within my first year. Then, in 1986, everything that was going so well crashed, the proverbial valley. At the time, I was pretty stubborn, so I figured I would keep doing what I was doing and eventually work out of it. I would just need to work a little harder.

I was in control. I doubled my efforts and worked harder, but the harder I worked, the more things seemed to be falling apart. I'm a pretty stubborn guy, so it took me about four years in that valley. I finally came to a place one interesting day because it happened to be a particularly bad day. I was on my way to a business meeting, and a month before that, a friend of my mom's had given me the Bible on cassette. I didn't know this dude, but apparently from a conversation he had with my mom, he knew I needed to start looking into that.

I was brought up Catholic, so I knew all the stories. But I knew Jesus like I knew George Washington or Abraham Lincoln, you know, historical figures. On this particular day, I'm driving to a meeting, so I figured I'd listen to one of those tapes. I didn't wanna waste my time, so I went to the very last tape to hear how it all ends, and I thought I'd be good and wouldn't need the rest of the tapes.

I took out the last tape, which was *Revelations*, the last book of the *Bible*. I put it in, and it started at chapter five, talking about, "Before the throne of God, there's 10,000 times 10,000 people that are worshipping God." And I'm hearing this, and it's upsetting me. So much so, I pulled over my car on the side of the road. I said to God, "How could you make us suffer this whole lifetime, and then to die and have to worship you for eternity?"

On the side of the road, my anger went to frustration where I just said to God that I was trying to run my life but was making a mess of it. "You gotta know better than me how to do my life. I'm done; I'm finished. I'm waiting on you and I'm going to bang on your door every day," I said to God. And that's what I did.

At that moment, Deantè, angels didn't appear or anything like that. I just made a promise to God that I was going to wait for Him.

Weeks later, I was in a church service, and I was a C and E Christian back then, meaning "Christmas and Easter." One of the Pastors was leaving for a different state. My mom really liked this guy, and she wanted me to go because it was his last service. "Amazing Grace" was playing, and I started having negative thoughts. I said, "Nope, I'm not going there, God. I'm waiting for you." Suddenly, I was blown away. It was like the presence of God just came over me, which I never felt before. I knew it was the Holy Spirit, and I was so stupefied that I didn't even remember the rest of the service.

In fact, my wife Nancy tells me that at the end of the service, I just walked out. I forgot to take her with me, and she had ridden there with me! I drove for twenty or thirty minutes in this presence. That day changed everything, and I did a 180 in my life. Everything that was important before—building my business, my kingdom—became irrelevant. I encountered something that was so much greater than anything heretofore in my life.

So, my focus became all about Him, all about God. All about what He wanted instead of what I wanted. That moment was such a 180 that I went back to cassette one and started listening to the whole Bible. Shortly thereafter, I got involved in youth ministry, working with teenagers. At the time, God's kingdom was up here, and business was down here. I decided that all I wanted to do was serve God.

It lasted until 2005, when I made an agreement with Marcus Smith to be a partner, and the rest is history. Nobody likes to be in a valley. Nobody likes to have those tumultuous times, adversities, and storms in their lives. But without me giving up on me…it was as if God pressed the pause button in my life. As I look back, I wouldn't have done that any differently. I see that as a time that changed everything because, had I not had that moment, that valley in my life—"failure," if you wanna call it that, along with having the modicum of success I have today, I might've thought it was all me.

I realized that having everything turned around was really about Him and serving God. The rest of the stuff was cool. The money, the recognition and all that, but that wasn't my mission anymore; that was a symptom of a better mission. So, to me, that was a huge failure that took me off the throne of my own life and changed everything.

Deantè: Do you believe that being in that valley was a test to see if you were a believer or if you had the resolve to keep pushing forward?

James: I would probably disagree with that because I had faith in God, but He wasn't in my top three priorities. I think that was orchestrated by God to shape my world so that I walked in the fullness of my true destiny and not on this off ramp, which would've left me very dissatisfied. I believe God breathes greatness into everybody, but sadly, so many people live the entirety of their lives and never walk in the fullness of their greatness. I've heard it said that there's nothing sadder for the world and for you than not living the life that you were meant to live. As I mentioned, I think that God pressed the "pause" button on my life long enough that the "horizontal" of my world was totally broken. If I looked to the left or to the right for answers, they were not there. I had to look vertically, so He got me into a place where I had nowhere to go other than Him, and that's where realignment happened.

Deantè: *Winning usually requires a lot of trial and error. On your journey so far, what were some of your biggest challenges to get you to where you are now?*

James: I'm asked that question a lot, Deantè. When I'm doing meetings and Q&As at different agencies around the country, I hear that all the time, and the answer comes to me right away because it's a no-brainer. My biggest challenge was me; I had to get over "self." It's a difficult thing to do because we all look through glasses of self. What happens to us during the day, how it impacts us, and what people say—everything is self.

When I was confronted with the selfishness that happens as we tried to build our own kingdom, I started trying to see other people and to seek to serve. I wanted to move from selfish to selfless. When you're selfless and being selfish, it's like a prison because everything is thought of in terms of yourself. So, you keep living the same experiences over and over again. You think about things that happen to you the same way, and there's no new ideas or thoughts because everything is locked in. When you break out of that and start being selfless and serving others with a mission greater than yourself, you truly have new adventures, challenges, and accomplishments.

For me, it changed everything, and it was a challenge, but I'll tell you this: it's not anything you win in a day…it's a daily battle of "self." When you can get glasses that look outward rather than inward and you start seeing other people and have a mission greater than you where you're serving others, it's a game changer. When you're on the top of the triangle of your life, it's like a roller coaster ride. If the mission is you, not every day is a good day. You don't accomplish that mission of benefitting yourself every day, just like in sales. One day, you're the king of sales. The next day, you can't put two sentences together to sell anything, right? But if your mission is to serve others, you're one hundred percent successful.

I've heard it said, "Don't count the success of the day by the harvest you reap, but rather by the seeds that you sow." So, that's what it's all about, and I often tell our sales organization, "Just serve the people and take the pressure off of yourself. You will be so relaxed that you'll be yourself." There's power in that which comes from understanding that your mission is a good mission. When the mission is ourselves, there's something inside us that knows it's selfish, making it hard to have passion for it. You may have "want" and "desire," but passion is birthed out of a powerful belief. It's hard to believe in just amassing your own big bank account or cars. But when you have a mission greater than yourself and you're serving others, you can believe in and have a passion for it. You'll have so much more success because of that belief.

If there was a doorway to your potential, it would be marked "Belief," and that belief is a precursor to passion—and passion is what moves you to greater levels of yourself that you haven't walked in yet. And most of life I think, Deantè, is really trying to garner as much of your potential as you can. We'll never live long enough to reach the end of our potential, right? But a lot of the challenge of life and the exciting part is moving more into that potential, and the only way you're going to do that is having a firm 100% belief in your mission.

History books are replete with names of individuals who have done amazing things to change the world. But when you desire to do great things, there's a lot of push back. If you have a belief and a passion, you're undaunted by whatever comes against you. You just press through, break through, and accomplish more; "Change the world" stuff!

Deantè: *How do you find out your purpose for your mission?*

James: I think one of the biggest problems people have these days is their own identity, who they are, what their purpose is. Many people are walking around with amnesia and have no idea who they are. I try to explain to our people about their identity, and I give them examples such as, "Take the universe...God created the universe, and every time scientists feel that they've found the end of the universe, someone invents a better telescope, and they find another galaxy and another million stars. And then there's the universe of the small. Every time they think they discovered the smallest thing, somebody invents a better microscope and finds something smaller that makes up that universe."

And so there's two vast universes; the greatest thing God created was us. In the book of Genesis, we were the only thing He created in His image. Think about that...the Creator of all things, He created us to be in His image. How much power is in that? So many people base their abilities and worth on the "horizontal" of the world, not understanding the "vertical" idea. They base their life and the things they can do and how they think about themselves on what other people have said based upon their past failures. So, they have a vision of themselves as a person who may have failed many times, or a person that others have said this or that about. They have no understanding of the greatness that God breathed into them. We're supposed to be world changers, but the idea is "If you don't have faith and belief that you are a world changer, that God made you in His image, that He breathed life into you, that He breathed greatness into you"—if you don't understand that, you're going to live your life in that "horizontal" zone and you'll never accomplish the things you're supposed to accomplish.

A lot of great things in life are done because of the understanding of who we are. We are not meant to be CEOs of our life. It's meant to be a partnership between us and God. Remember, the State of Ohio's motto is, "With God, all things are possible." To understand your purpose and your mission is to understand yourself, and a famous philosopher said, "Know thyself."

Deantè: *There is a perception that we have to be confident in order to achieve difficult things. I believe courage is more important than confidence, but what experience comes to mind when you were afraid to try something because maybe you lacked belief in yourself?*

James: I still lack belief in myself, and let me explain that. I don't lack belief in the spirit of God that's in me. But my humanity, I always have to check myself. Always. And it doesn't mean I don't admire the gifts and abilities God's given me. He gifts all of us and a lot of life is figuring out which gift I have and which one I don't. When you say "belief in" myself, sometimes I can't trust myself to be perfectly honest. I can't trust my humanity, my selfishness—but I *can* trust He who is in me. So, I consult Him often because so many times, I am way off and I'm not thinking how I should be thinking. It's a daily thing, and it's like we have to keep coming to God to get the default back to the path that He lays before us.

My favorite Proverbs, chapter three, verse five/six: "Trust in the Lord. Lean not on your own understanding but acknowledge Him and He'll set your path straight." Part of that, "lean not on the reality of the moment," because in our humanness, our perception is sometimes way off. I want to see with His eyes, not my own, because my own eyes deceive me. But in every situation, I want to as it says, "Trust in Him" and "don't lean" on whatever is happening in the moment because it might give me a false perception of truth. But if you acknowledge God, He'll set the path straight; that is key to me.

Bringing it down to a worldly level, in building a business, there's a lot of fears that can happen causing you to freeze in inaction. When you're frozen in inaction, you're going to lose in that situation. The hardest part of being a leader is being the decision maker because you're responsible for the results of that decision, and that will freeze many into not making a decision, which is the wrong decision.

I remember very clearly sitting at my desk one day pondering the decisions I had to make. And these were decisions when I was building the business, so I didn't have any money. I was in red ink and... just trying to survive. When you're in survival mode, you make bad decisions; it's not a growth mode. So, as I was pondering this stuff, an idea came into my head: "What would I do differently or what decision would I make if I already had a million dollars in the bank?"

That idea was key to me because I was no longer making decisions out of fear of loss because I already had, right? Instead, I was making smarter decisions based on wisdom and growth, rather than survival. If you're in survival mode and you just try to stay comfortable, know that "Comfort is the enemy of destiny," So, when I'm in that comfort or survival mode, I'm not getting to where I want to get by moving up higher levels. That was a big thing to trick my mind to believing I had already made it and already had the money in the bank, so what decision should I make for somebody who already had a million dollars? That helped me make better decisions.

Deantè: *I think it's very enlightening to know that you don't always have self-belief because you seem so focused on doing things that you've done before and it's given you all this extra belief.*

James: There's a lot to be said for experience. Probably the first time I entered this situation, I had a certain amount of fear and trepidation. As you work through it and you learn through experience, the key thing is learning because adversity produces fear. I tell my people that adversity wasn't meant to push us down as much as it was meant to elevate us. As I look back on my life, I see that in the valleys I learned so much more than on top of the mountain. Because we're molded and shaped in the valleys, but the problem is, most people are only looking at the top of the mountain wishing they were there instead of looking in the valley and finding the buried treasure buried. I think the valley is where you get what you don't have to elevate yourself to a higher level.

There's something you need to get to the higher level, and not only get there, but maintain that level.

Deantè: *What advice would you give someone who is afraid to try something because they are afraid that they might fail?*

James: I'd ask them, "What would you do differently today if an angel and the Lord appeared to you and told you that everything you do today, you will not fail?" What would you do differently if you knew you couldn't fail? People tell me they believe, but when I ask that question, most are like, "Oh man, I'd do this and do that and have more appointments…" and I say, "Live your life that way. Wake up every morning and feel that you cannot fail today." You expect and anticipate miracles to happen today, good things, Deantè. Most people live in the past and feel like today will be the same as yesterday; the same disappointments, the same failures, and guess what? They walk into the same disappointments and the same failures because that's what they anticipate and expect.

I always tell people, "Don't address the darkness, pronounce the light." In other words, when you wake up in the morning, anticipate and expect good things. Yesterday is the enemy of today, and many people that have never had a failure would think anything could happen today, right? When we were kids, we were asked what we wanted to be when we grew up. We could do anything and be anything! But because of life, we take these punches until what we believe we can do becomes smaller and smaller until we're in this self-imposed prison shackled to a wall and we think the day will be the same, but it's not.

People dwell on the past, so I try to help people get rid of what's holding them back in their head. I've met the enemy, and the enemy is me. It's our thought process. The challenge is to take twenty-four hours and think about what you think about, and you will discover all the negativity, all the recounting of past offenses, past abuses, past failures. Literally, it robs you of the beauty and the purity and the freshness of this day.

24.
HALA TAHA:
Rejection is Redirection

CEO, YAP Media Marketing and Podcast Agency | Host of the Young and Profiting podcast | 3 years in business

Hala Taha made a powerful impression on me the first time we interacted on LinkedIn nearly three years ago. She was warm, friendly, and full of positive energy—all of which explains how and why she has become one of the most driven and fearless entrepreneurs in the world. The battle scars she earned in the cutthroat entertainment industry have fueled her stratospheric rise to eminence, and she's just getting started. It is my privilege to present to you Hala Taha.

—D.Y.

Deantè: Based on your life experiences, how important has failure been to your success?

Hala: Failure has been one of the most important things to my success, and I think all of my successes have come on the heels of failure. The biggest failure I had was when I was working at Hot 97. I interned there free for three years. Although I was not technically an employee, I was essentially a manager at the station, and I managed other interns that would come and go. I did research, ran the contest commercials, and was on air. I was basically the assistant of all the DJs as well a personal assistant to Angie Martinez. I worked my butt off and dropped out of school for the opportunity. In the radio world, it's common for people to be unpaid apprentices for many years and make their money off the brand of the station.

Three years into it, I was getting a lot of pressure from my family that I wasn't being paid and they were taking advantage of me. I stood up for myself and said, "I at least wanna get paid minimum wage. I'm here every single day, and I see other people getting hired," but they continued not paying me, which was a little strange. So, after standing up for myself, Angie Martinez basically fired me and my key card access was disabled. I was devastated. I was no longer in college, and my parents were fed up with me for working for free at the station for so long.

Not only did I lose my job, but I was practically blackballed by the industry. Angie Martinez told all the DJs not to pick up my calls anymore. People told me that they couldn't associate with me anymore...like basically I was on the shit list. I lost all my contacts from my adult work experience, so...they really screwed me up. But within four days, I had a new idea. I was fired on a Thursday, and by Sunday, I thought up *The Sorority of Hip-Hop*, an entertainment news blog providing a platform for women who would stand together and have their own voice. Nobody could tell us "No," and we would support each other, lift each other up, and share each other's audiences.

And so, I recruited girls from Def Jam and iHeart and VH-1... just all over the industry from radio, TV, and media. Within three months, we were one of the most popular hip-hop and R&B sites in the world. The same DJs who didn't wanna pay me minimum wage were now calling me up to host parties with them. Angie Martinez came crawling back trying to get me on *Love and Hip-Hop* and introduce me to Mona Scott. It's like everything got flipped around, and I went from being an intern to everybody's peer all because I failed and took control over my own life. And every time I failed really, really bad, I would step back and feel like, "Oh, I have this new purpose that I need to go there on my own." I definitely think failure is a huge part of success.

Deantè: *Wow. That story is spine-tinglingly amazing. Out of curiosity, where do you think you were able to summon that resolve and resilience from after being devastated about being fired?*

Hala: I think it's because I feel like I've had to work ten times as hard as anybody else to get any sort of achievement. I was in middle school when 9/11 happened, and I remember being a popular kid, into sports and always had a lead in the play, was invited over to friends' houses all the time. When 9/11 happened, suddenly, I wasn't allowed to be in the talent show. I never made any sports teams after that, and it was really hard. People were scared of Arabic people and my family went from being normal to being weird. I feel like I had a lack of opportunities in high school, but my ambition never went away. I would always still be that kid who would try out for everything and never make anything.

I attended college at a really diverse school in Newark, New Jersey, and everybody was ethnic. It didn't matter that I was Arabic, and I was given the opportunities as everyone else. In college, I made the cheerleading squad, was the lead in the play, and was top in my sorority. I wasn't scared of trying because I had already experienced so much rejection, so that didn't hurt me anymore. I took more risks than others after developing a thick skin from all of the rejection as a teenager. I guess I'm lucky that it didn't completely kill my confidence.

Deantè: *Well, that's very, very impressive, and we can all learn from your story. Now, winning usually requires a lot of trial and error. On your journey so far, what were some of your biggest challenges to get to where you are now?*

Hala: When I first started my podcast, people asked me, "Why would you do that? Why would you spread yourself so thin?" I was told that I should start a family, not a podcast because the market was too saturated and I would jeopardize my career. I heard that from my co-workers, my lover at the time, and even my family and friends. My friends thought I was starting a podcast because I was unhappy in my relationship; it's as if nobody could believe that I wanted to start a podcast because it was my passion and I felt strongly about it.

So, I think one of the challenges was navigating the noise and following what I thought was my destiny. It's difficult, especially when you're a people-pleaser who wants to make people happy and avoid conflict. But at the same time, you need to stand up for yourself and follow your dreams. Staying on my path when I felt like many people didn't want me to be was a big challenge. I jeopardized and lost many relationships with friends and others who couldn't accept that I would no longer have every weekend free to hang out with them anymore.

Anything worth having requires a lot of hard work and a lot of hours, and I definitely worked late nights and through the weekends to get to where I am today. I think that has impacted my relationships somewhat and helped me build even stronger relationships with those who are more aligned with the type of life that I want to live.

Another challenge is scaling. There are now sixty-three people working at *Young and Profiting* podcast, which is a big team, and that grew in a year. We started with ten volunteers, and by episode two, I had Timothy Tan, who's my business partner. By episode eight, I had ten volunteers who were just fans of the show on a Slack channel, and now we're up to sixty-three paid team members.

It all started from people working for free because they believed in the mission, in me, and in the service that we're providing the world with our content. A lot of those volunteers are still with us and are now team leads and some have quit their full-time jobs. But getting out of the volunteer culture now that we're a real business with high profile clients and getting people to step into their roles and also having to figure out the volunteers that stayed with us aren't gonna be the ones who are gonna take us to the next level...it's just hard to scale your team into a regular work culture.

It's just growing pains because we went from a passion project to a very fast-growing marketing agency.

Deantè: *Wow. That is actually amazing and I'm very proud of you.*

Hala: Thanks!

Deantè: *There is a perception that we have to be confident to achieve difficult things. I believe that courage is more important than confidence, but what experiences come to mind when maybe you lacked self-belief because maybe you didn't think you could do something?*

Hala: I feel like that's the opposite of who I am. I almost never think I can't do something. There are certainly things I don't *want* to do. For example, I would never try out to be a ballet dancer because I don't have the skills. But if I have the relevant skills, or if I feel that it's realistic for me to learn what I need to learn, I usually feel confident enough to do it. I understand that you'll never be 100% ready for anything, and skills are transferable. If I feel that I have skills that will help me along the way, I don't need to know every single thing.

I've also learned that not feeling ready is mostly a vocabulary problem. If you have Imposter syndrome or anything similar, it's usually a glossary problem— you need to learn fifty words so that you can understand conversations going on around you. Or you might need to learn different acronyms or phrases specific to the industry. Once you know those fifty words, things start to click and make a lot more sense. You can talk the jargon and become more confident, so I'm never afraid to learn. I know things can happen even later on in life. I never thought I would get back into entertainment; I thought I would be in corporate forever, and there were four or five years when I didn't touch a mic.

When I started the *Young and Profiting* podcast, I had forgotten how to do interviews and it was like starting all over again, even though I had years of experience. I see what happened then with trying one last time and making it, so I also feel like I will have my own salon or makeup company at some point, and I'm not afraid to learn that either. I know it's completely different, but it's fun to learn new things, and I look at it as a fun challenge.

Deantè: *That's a lot of fearlessness and most of us would be shaking in our boots, but you go the opposite way. That's pretty powerful. Last question, what advice would you give to someone who is afraid to try because maybe they fear they might fail at something?*

Hala: You have to enjoy the journey and the process. If you are talented, motivated, and willing to roll up your sleeves, you will get more at-bats and more opportunities, or even obstacles, that are part of your journey to success. People believe obstacles block their success, but it's actually their path, and if somebody tells you "No," take a turn. When somebody else says "No," take another turn. Figure out your turns and you'll gain experience so that one day you end up where you really belong.

Your experiences will give you all the skills and knowledge you need, even if they were short-lived or resulted in failure. It's all a part of becoming who you're supposed to be, so I would suggest you say "Yes" to things as often as you can, especially if you know that you're a "No" person. If you always say "No" to trying things, make an effort to say "Yes" more often. Don't see opportunities as winning or losing, but as gaining experience you can carry with you for other opportunities. Hopefully, you'll land on something that makes you feel really fulfilled.

25.
MICHAEL VASU: Sacrifice Creates Opportunity

State General Agent, Owner of Vasu Agency of American Income Life | Nearly 16 years in business

Michael Vasu has convinced me that he is a genius. Not because he says so, because he doesn't. His genius is based on the fact that he will be the first to tell anyone that he doesn't know everything. In my opinion, that's why he knows as much as he does. He's a mental tactician, a student of life, and he possesses a surreal confluence of personality and gratitude that allows him to change the world, one person at a time. It is my privilege to present to you Michael Vasu.

—D.Y.

Deantè: *Based on your life experiences, how important has failure been to your success?*

Michael: I know it sounds cliche, but it's been instrumental for many reasons. You have a tendency to grow more in the valley than you do at the mountaintop. So, when things are good and you're having success, you start wondering, *"Why am I having success? How is this even happening? I just don't wanna mess it up."*

When things are going well, most people tend not to want to mess with whatever's happening, so they don't grow as much. It's not always about ego; sometimes it is. If you think you're "all that," you're not going to be open to coaching, and you're not going to be humble. So, the times I've been in the valley or where the objective of the goal that I've set for myself is big, I'm naturally going to be the underdog.

I must become more creative and learn how I got somewhere or how I can get out of there, which gets the wheels turning in my brain to become more solutions-oriented. I have had failures, and I anticipate that I will have more. The only person not failing is the one not doing anything.

At one time, my brother let himself go and wasn't taking care of himself or eating well. I asked, "Chris, what are you gonna do to turn this thing around?" He replied, "What you don't realize is that I'm actively working on my *before* picture, so it will be more dramatic when I turn this thing around." Sometimes I think that way; the bigger your goals, the more dramatic the rise. And putting yourself at a disadvantage almost always brings out the best in you.

Deantè: *That is phenomenal. Clearly, you've had a lot of setbacks, and you wouldn't trade them for the world.*

Michael: I wouldn't. But there are some I wish I could go back and, knowing what I know now, avoid them. Still, there would be no way for me to know what I know now if I didn't experience those failures. So, they're part of my journey, and unless you're really young or you've lived a very charmed life, you will have disappointments, regrets, and setbacks. I don't think there's a way to avoid those aside from not living. Don't play it so safe that you remain stagnant your whole life.

I've had personal and professional failures and have experienced things that I never thought I would experience. But you have a choice in life; get back up, learn from those mistakes, and get better. Or just stay there and be a victim, claiming there's nothing you can do about your circumstances. You and I both know that's not true.

Deantè: Winning usually requires a lot of trial and error. On your journey so far, what have been some of your biggest challenges to get to where you are right now?

Michael: The one common thread in all the challenges that I've faced is *me*. I've been there for all the disappointments and failures, so I think the biggest challenge is managing yourself, your attitude, goals, vision, and objectives because they're yours. You are with yourself 24/7 365, from your first breath 'til your last breath. Because you know yourself intimately, you can rationalize things to yourself, talk yourself in and out of things, and compromise on your goals by justifying things. They say that knowledge is power, but sometimes knowledge of yourself can be a real weakness.

I think back in my life and pretty much all the failures I've had were either because I justified things to myself, told myself that things were okay when they weren't, or I just simply wasn't good enough and my growth didn't start until I said, *"You know what? I just don't know how to handle this."* In business, I had to tell myself "I'm not a good enough leader to handle this." The growth started when I had a moment of sobriety saying, "Here's the fact: we are where we are. I'm trying, but I'm not good enough. How do I become good enough?"

Once you turn that realization into a question, your brain starts working and points to solutions. You start surrounding yourself with the people you need to be around. You start to mitigate weaknesses and play towards your strengths and learn the skills you need to overcome it. In my life, I can go back to the time when I was a little boy and the challenge of assimilation growing up in an immigrant family. When I went to kindergarten, I didn't speak English, so I was always an outsider and an outcast in a lot of ways. It wasn't my parents' fault because they did the best they could. It wasn't the other kids' fault because when you're five years old, you don't have the emotional IQ to say "Hey, this guy is a little bit weird, but he can't do nothin' about it. It's just the way that he is."

I tried to fit in and wanted to fit in from a young age, but felt that my parents, who were strict, were holding me back. A lot of the kids that I gravitated towards were ones you'd maybe call the "bad kids" in school. They always seemed a lot cooler to me, especially because of my strict home environment. I thought, "Oh, I wanna be a little bit more of a rebel," and I have a little rebelliousness in me naturally. I'm not a big fan of trying to be like anybody else; I wanna be just who I am so, sometimes that's caused me to fail. But if I wouldn't have gone down that path, I would not have developed my own instinct and way of doing things.

I often say, "I'd rather lose *my* way than win *your* way if I don't believe in your way." If I'm not sold on it, I'm not going down that path. I've spent fifteen and a half years—I'm 39, so fifteen and a half years is a big chunk of my life—in business. I've been in business about as long as I was in school from kindergarten all the way through graduate school.

School was the first education that I received, and I look at what I'm learning in business as education. I think prosperity will come in the future, and I'm okay with that because I don't do this for the rewards; I do it for the responsibility. One failure that I've learned is when you get too comfortable with rewards and start to tie your personality to success and money, things that come and go, you have a hard time recovering from that.

And so, you learn that you can't tie your success to rewards, accolades, trophies, or money because those things are fleeting. The truth is that I want to be prosperous, but it's just not something I'm chasing; it's something I would rather attract and not change who I am. I wanna change who I am so that I can become the magnet for the kind of success that I wanna have. You can chase it for a season, a month, a quarter, or a year. Then, usually, you'll get tired of chasing it. So, as I've gotten older, I try to switch my focus to "Who do I need to become as a person, how do I become the best version of me to attract the rewards that I'm supposed to attract?"

That may sound non-committal, but I don't know what the rewards are. Sometimes in life, God doesn't bless you with certain things like financial success because maybe if at that moment he did, it could wreck your life. It may have to come at a different time, so I trust His timing, and I trust His judgement. I don't try to put myself on the level of God's wisdom to say I know as much as He does; I can only do what I can do and based on His judgement when the right time comes, I'll take the blessings.

Deantè: *You're saying that you believe things happen when they're supposed to happen?*

Michael: Yes. I think that if you're doing the right things and you're not chasing the rewards, they come when they're supposed to come. Sometimes, we're so focused and so obsessed with chasing the good, we completely miss the great that would be there by continuing on the journey and the path God has us on.

Deantè: *What experience comes to mind during your life where you were afraid to try something because you lacked belief in yourself?*

Michael: There aren't a lot of times where I think to myself, "I can't do that." That's not part of my DNA. What *is* part of my DNA is more likely "I probably can't do it, but..." Look, if I'm on the street and I run into Connor McGregor, and I look at him the wrong way and I piss the guy off, guess what? He's probably a much better fighter than me, but that doesn't mean if he tries to fight me, I'm not going to try to fight back. Now I may not win the fight, but I know I can fight back.

In life, the consequences are probably not so immediate as getting into a fight with Connor McGregor. Life may hit me, but it doesn't mean that I can't fight back, and through that struggle and fighting back, I begin to develop my fighting skills. And the good news is, I'm not getting punched in the face and don't get a black eye or a bloody nose. I have the opportunity to learn.

One example that I use a lot is growing up in a household where my dad worked two and three jobs my whole life, I didn't do a lot of projects around the house with him. I'm not a super handy guy, but I am a really committed guy. If I tell you that I'm gonna do something, I will do that even if it harms me sometimes. I'll never forget installing a hose reel in the garage of my first house years ago when I had no idea what I was doing.

I knew that if I bought the hose reel, the hose, and the parts that I needed, I could figure it out. Sure, I could've paid a guy a hundred bucks to install this thing, and by the time I went back and forth to Home Depot three, four times to get the drills that I needed and get all the parts and pieces, it probably cost me $300. But I committed myself to doing it, so there was no backing out. Does that make sense? If I were to install another hose reel, which I would never do because one of the ways that I stimulate the economy is hiring people to do this stuff, but if I were to install another hose reel, I know for a fact that I know how to do it because I've done it once.

As an example, I've never installed a ceiling fan, but if I told you that I was going to install a ceiling fan, I'm gonna die before that thing doesn't get installed. It might take me five or six hours, but between YouTube, Phone-a-Friend, or FaceTime, I'm gonna figure it out somehow, some way. Now, if I install a second, third, fourth, or fifth ceiling fan, by the fifth one, it's not gonna take me five hours...because I've got experience. So, what I'm always trying to gain are skills and experience. I don't care about the rewards; those can come later. When I'm trying to grow and go to the next level, I assume that I'm getting no rewards because I'm not good at this level, yet — but I will be. I believe that I can fight back, and if I fight back long enough, I'll learn how to fight and will beat this game.

That's how my brain works; I really don't have a fear because most of the things that I've done, I didn't know how to do. But when your brain goes into "solutions mode," and says, "Let me get this skill, let me get the experience," I feel like you can overcome pretty much anything.

Deantè: *That's exceptional because it seems to be the exception to the rule for most people. Where do you think that mentality came from? It sounds like it goes back to your childhood.*

Michael: My parents were really strict, and had very high expectations because they had made a huge sacrifice to come to the United States. Imagine the best opportunity in the world was in China, you don't have much money or much of anything else, and you say, "This is such a great place. As long as I show up there, even though I don't have a job, don't know anyone, and don't speak the language, I can provide the best opportunity for my kids here." And you show up in China, and you have to learn Chinese, figure out how to get a job, and learn the culture and all this stuff…"

Watching your parents do something like that takes away your excuse to say, "Well I don't like to be uncomfortable." How comfortable do you think it was for them? They came for opportunity, so growing up, my parents said, "Look, we have these jobs that don't pay a lot of money. But we're gonna work a lot of hours and we're gonna do whatever we need to do to put you through school. Your end of the bargain is getting straight A's. A 'B' is unacceptable; we're not going to tell you that it's good because you tried, and we just wanna be really clear about that.

"Don't tell us you're not good at math or English or whatever; you'll learn it. You're gonna have to work harder at it so that you can be the best that you can be, which to us, is an 'A' on your report card." My parents didn't accept the idea of weaknesses or that I might've had ADD. I'm not being insensitive; I'm just telling you that this was my experience.

Deantè: What advice would you give someone who is afraid to try something because they are afraid that they might fail?

Mike: I think whatever you're trying to achieve, the only downside is time. You could potentially use time and not achieve your goal, but in the process of reaching for a goal, you develop yourself. Life is more about who you become than what you get because who you become allows you to be a servant to other people. When we all die, at our funerals, nobody is going to talk about what we got; they're gonna talk about what we gave and the impact that we made on others.

And so, what I would tell them is "If you're not doing something about what you want to attain, you've already lost because the worst-case scenario is that nothing changes after you go after it. You will lose a little time, but you'll gain a little experience. You will probably be a better version of yourself and you will be tougher. The higher the level that you want to achieve in life, the greater the chances of failure. But that reveals to yourself where your proficiency is, and you know you need to work on certain areas of your life so you can become better. Your next stab at it, you're probably gonna do a lot better and better and better.

So, I would say that the greatest failure is not trying because then you're not giving yourself a chance to change your circumstances, and you're going to stay where you are. The worst-case scenario of trying is that nothing changes, so you really only have an upside. Most successful people I know have failed a lot. J.K. Rowling, author of the *Harry Potter* books, got turned down by thirty or forty publishing companies. Imagine if she would've stopped. Think about the joy that those books have brought into people's lives and the amount of revenue that's been generated from the movies, books, and different products related to that.

If the universe continues to push against you, that's not a sign you should give up; it's a sign that you should try harder. In a moment of difficulty, in a moment of challenge, most people cower and give up. That's when it's calling on you to use all of your strength, genius, wisdom, resources, and relationships. If you do, it's very difficult to lose or fail completely.

Deantè: Man! I feel like I'm hearing you speak for the first time, and this is probably like the two hundredth time. That was phenomenal, man...so many quotables!

Mike: I think there's something to be said about being driven towards something in life. That's what really makes someone a man or a woman-- an adult, is saying, "This is what I'm striving for. This is what I'm reaching for." I think you must embrace life the way you have it and celebrate it the way you have it. The basis for being great is being grateful.

26.
JOHN WRIGHT:
THE WRIGHT WAY IS YOUR WRIGHT SOLUTION

President and Founder of HWA Alliance of CPA Firms | 36 years in business

John Wright seemed to be quite intimidating when I met him eight years ago. It took almost no time to discover that he has a wonderful sense of humor and a focus that many business executives wish they possessed. While interviewing him for this book, I gained a greater appreciation for the enormous challenges he endured on the path to his current excellence. He is one of my biggest inspirations, and it is my privilege to present to you John Wright.

—D.Y.

Deantè: Based on your life experiences, how important has failure been to your success?

John: I tend not to characterize it as failure, but in some circles, people do call it that. I call it growth. There are ups and downs in business, so you can call it failure because I've had to file bankruptcy twice in my life. At certain points, I thought I would go out of business, and I didn't know where the next dollar would come from. There were times when I didn't know if I would be able to make payroll, and fortunately, I've never missed a payroll. Thinking about that question, I guess failure *has* been a part of my journey. At one point, I owned rental properties and several assets, but lost everything and had to rebuild.

There was a time when I lost my business and my biggest client and had to rebuild. I've had to rebuild several times and I've made many sacrifices in that rebuilding process. You could call those failures, but I think of it as part of my growth journey. Without those setbacks, I probably wouldn't be where I am today. Sometimes you have to reset and go in a different direction. I consider going out of business and getting a job that was never on my radar as a failure. I used to have nightmares about going back to my previous job, which would have been a complete failure to me!

Deantè: *What was your previous job that was such a nightmare?*

John: It was a great job, but it was the idea of having a job. I spent ten years at NASA, and that was the first real job that I had. There, I had my initial education and exposure to prejudice and discrimination. It was a great job, but I was surrounded by rednecks who made it a nightmare.

Deantè: *That had to be terrifying!*

John: NASA was a great job. Failure to me would've been crawling back on my knees and asking for my job back.

Deantè: *Winning usually requires a lot of trial and error. What were some challenges you faced to get you where you are right now?*

John: Being a Black man in America is probably the biggest challenge because just being a black man throws up roadblocks on its own that Caucasians don't really have to face. Lack of capital and banking finance was an issue, and I had to be very creative to overcome those things. Because of our history and the way black people think, you couldn't take it for granted that the community would support you in your efforts.

In some cases, the community were the very ones trying to tear you down, so at some point, you always hit that brick wall. After leaving NASA, I spent a few years at Ernst & Young, where I encountered a different type of racism. It was more institutionalized, and the people were more sophisticated and educated, so they weren't going to call you "nigger," not even under their breath. But they treated you pretty much the same, so you had to overcome that. Once I started my own practice, I was still relegated to dealing with black people as my clients because the doors to the majority community were closed to us.

It took several years for us to break through those barriers. Now, we have almost as many white clients as minority clients, which comes from being in the business for so long and building a reputation and brand. It's not completely colorblind, but it is moving slowly in that direction. If you're good at what you do, people just accept you. But as we've seen recently with all of the protests about criminal justice, we still have a long way to go.

Deantè: *What experience comes to mind when you were afraid to try something because you lacked self-belief or you didn't think you could achieve it?*

John: I mentioned racism before because you become conditioned to it and avoid venturing out and trying to grow, anticipating barriers will be thrown up against you. There is a lot of fear when applying for a business loan, knowing they would scrutinize you more than a comparable majority business. Also, once I started acquiring Caucasian clients, I was a little reluctant to walk into a boardroom and make a presentation to only white men.

When I was just 18, I applied for a job as an electrician. I was extremely intimidated to go before the board and fearful to walk into a room with only white guys, but I had to overcome that fear. Now that I'm older and wiser, I'm no longer intimidated because my skills, knowledge, and business acumen have increased over time, minimizing the fear. I don't fear anything at this point.

Deantè: *What advice would you give someone who is afraid to try something because they are afraid to fail?*

John: Fear is good. If you were interviewing a bona fide hero or somebody that committed a tremendous act of self-sacrifice for others, they will probably tell you they were afraid. Fear is always in the back of your mind, but it is a good thing. Embrace it, but you don't allow it to control you. You must control it.

Fear causes you to be cautious. Every time you take a step in the dark, you overcome that fear a little and start building your confidence. You can't overcome it all at once; you may need to take baby steps like being afraid you'll fall when learning how to walk. But you know it's worth learning, so you take that one shaky step and then another until you can let go of your parents and just keep going.

Once you take that first step, eventually, you'll be running and will forget all about your fear.

27.
DEANTÈ YOUNG: ONE MONKEY DON'T STOP NO SHOW

Owner, Chief Creative Architect of Dirty Truth Publishing (a division of Dirty Truth Media) | Author | Entrepreneur | 1 year in business

Julius Chisholm is one of my trusted advisors, coaches, and friends, so it comes as no surprise to me that I entrusted him with interviewing me for my book. His questions were modified versions of my own for others in this book, but with his added twist. I'm grateful for his participation in the book, as well as for his excellent interviewing of me. It is my privilege to present to you, ME!

—D.Y.

Julius: How important has failure been to get you where you're at now?

Deantè: Failure has been extremely important, at least what society considers to be failure. I decided twenty years ago to look at things others believe to be failures as priceless teaching tools. My first major failure occurred when I was six years old, and it was the worst thing to ever happen to me to that point.

A kid who was three years older than me was trying to teach me how to ride a bicycle with no training wheels. And over two weeks, I kept falling, falling, falling, falling, and I cried each time. Everyone else seemed like they knew how to ride a bike, but not me. So, he kept giving me pep talks, but at six, you don't understand that. He would hold the bike and then let go, and I would just fall. After about two dozen falls, he told me that once he let go of the bike, I needed to start pedaling really fast, and I'd be able to keep my balance. He did that, and I kept my balance.

So, my first major lesson was that if I stopped every time I failed or every time I cried and didn't think I could do it, I would never get anywhere. The same thing happened ten years later while trying to get my driver's license. In driver's ed, I kept hitting the maneuverability poles, and I didn't think I would ever get my license. When I took the driving test, I scored perfectly on maneuverability but had points taken off the driving part, and I couldn't believe it.

Those things proved to me that failure is so important because you learn so much from it. You learn very little when you succeed.

Julius: *I like that. So, I'm going to circle back to something you mentioned about when your friend would hold the bike. He would hold the bike and he would let go, but he told you, "Hey, you need to pedal as fast as you can." We know with bikes that the faster, the better. They have two wheels and that accomplishes balance, right? But to me, that sounds like whatever you're doing, you should immerse yourself into it totally versus just paddling one paddle at a time, taking your sweet time, because that's when you fall off.*

For example, if I want to learn how to swim right, I might immerse myself in swimming. I'm gonna hang around swimmers and see what they're doing in practice. Given that example, how important is it to immerse yourself into whatever it is you're doing?

Deantè: It's critical because you're giving yourself a higher probability of achieving what you're trying to achieve by doing what others in that space are already doing.

Julius: You've obviously accomplished some things. This is your third book, and we all know that you don't get there without having challenges. What are some of the biggest challenges that got you to where you are now?

Deantè: The biggest challenge with writing books is making sure I create something other people will find useful. I tend to write books about things I know a lot about from personal experience and can fill in the blanks of what I don't know by doing research. I always want to make things that resonate with other people, and the challenge in writing books is to think of it not as me but as the reader. You want them to extrapolate everything they need to from what you're saying, but we have a tendency to believe that what we know is common knowledge, and it's not.

So, am I articulating this properly so the reader can understand where I'm coming from? I want this to be meaningful, and I want them to be able to say, "Man! I'm gonna try this." I need to speak it in the way that people need to hear it, which is the challenge and the ultimate goal. These books are not for me; they're for other people.

Julius: Would you agree that you need different perspectives? Because the only way to write a book for most people is actually to place yourself into their shoes.

Deantè: Yeah, that's what I do. When you try to serve everyone, you serve no one, so it's really just the target market, and that's kinda what I do. It helps my personal relationships, too.

For example, years ago, I had girlfriends who were so insecure when I would talk to other girls as friends, and I'd be like, "What are you concerned about? She's just my friend." But now, I ask myself, if I was her, how would I feel about that? And I never looked at it like that. I always looked at it from my point of view, which means that you can't help anybody if you're just looking at it from your point of view.

That's why you have to put yourself in the shoes of other people as best as you can. You're never gonna be able to do it fully, but as best as you can, and then you will be able to understand people a lot better.

Julius: That requires a level of maturity, right?

Deantè: Yes, definitely. You don't start out like that, though.

Julius: It also takes a level of maturity to handle failure correctly..

Deantè: And a great deal of self-awareness, which most lack.

Julius: What is your biggest challenge in life now?

Deantè: My mother's only son has always been my biggest challenge, by far. Seriously. Things that I didn't do until I was thirty, but should've done when I was eighteen, came because I have a mediocre side that wants to stay that way. So, the enemy is within, and we are all programmed that way. When we say, "Man I just went to the gym six days in a row, I can take a day off," that's your mediocre side begging for attention. So, I've been my own biggest challenge because I know what to do and I choose not to do it for whatever the "because" is. That has stuck its foot out and tripped me up many times.

The good thing is that I've been able to look at that and recognize it, and most people don't. America thinks that Nicki Minaj or Kim Kardashian has the biggest butt—the biggest "but" is the "but" in your head. You say, "Well, but..." and you've already lost.

Julius: There's a perception that you must have confidence before doing something, but I think courage is more important than confidence. Give some situations where you didn't feel 100% **confident***, but you still had the courage to tackle that task.*

Deantè: Writing my first book, I did not know so many things. I felt confident that I could pull it off, but I didn't feel confident in how I was gonna do a lot of different things. With faith and courage, I was able to push through. When it's something that you care a lot about, you'll get it done no matter what. I had no idea what it would cost or how I would finance it, but I felt very courageous doing this because I believe it's something the world needs. At the very least, it will lay the groundwork for me to become a symbol of transformation for others because I've gone through that myself, and continue to do so.

Julius: If you were talking to somebody who's afraid do something because of fear of failure, what advice would you give them?

Deantè: I would tell them something that my grandmother said. It's not about failure, but it correlates. She told me that, "One monkey don't stop no show." And that translates to this:

"one failed opportunity doesn't stop the march toward the ultimate opportunity you're trying to get." If I want a Heineken beer and I go to Convenient to buy one, but they're all out, I can go to Speedway, Giant Eagle...so that one "monkey," that one store, didn't stop me from getting what I wanted.

I would say that the real failure is failing by default, meaning not trying. I liked so many girls in the past, but I didn't believe I could get any of them, and I figured, "Why would she go for me?" So, I failed by default. It's so much better to swing the bat, and even if you just get lucky and hit it, that's a lot better than not trying because there's no chance or possibility of anything. So, "one monkey don't stop no show" means that one opportunity lost does not mean that all opportunities fall by the wayside.

I would tell people to do what's needed to be courageous and go for the gold. *The Wizard of Oz* is a perfect example of that. In the movie, Dorothy walked down the Yellow Brick Road and encountered several obstacles like poppies that put her to sleep and vicious flying monkeys. The Wicked Witch was against her and tried everything to stop her. Dorothy's goal to get home was very important to her, giving her the driving force to overcome all of the roadblocks in her way.

So, I would look at life as the proverbial Yellow Brick Road because of all the obstacles that you will face. But when you get to the "Emerald City," which is your ultimate destination, you will be so much better as a person because of what it made of you. Dorothy became stronger after going through many trials and tribulations. Of course, it ended up being a dream, but one worth having because she realized she had what she needed all along with a loving family around her.

Failing by default is the ultimate disaster.

Closing Thoughts

I wrote this book because it pisses me off that I've constantly let the fear of failure stop me from going after what I want. It's even more fucked up seeing other people repeating that same ridiculous mistake.

I'm here to help change that habit for you and me.

Stop putting people, things, and desires on a pedestal because that makes you feel you're not good enough for it or them.

The high achievers featured in this book didn't just fall out of bed one morning and become champions. They broke through their mental barrier of self-doubt and built themselves into a force of nature.

You have that power too!

Winning is For Losers! is the ultimate masterclass on clawing your way through life's sucker punches and land mines to eventually get what you want. Simply put, the people in this world who do the most winning are also the ones who've lost the most.

All because they dare to try and take calculated risks despite what the outcome *might* be. Yes, they "lose" more than anyone else, but it's never actually a "failure" because they gain priceless knowledge from experience.

My challenge to you is to start training yourself to take chances on trying shit that seems unlikely to go your way. Confidence is not necessary, but courage will push you through even when you don't believe in yourself.

If you manage to take those calculated risks and ignore the voice in your head that's telling you that you can't or won't succeed, you will eventually accomplish more than you ever thought possible.

Start that business. Ask that hottie who seems to be out of your league on a date. Ask for a much higher hourly wage during your job interview.

Embrace rejection. It will make you tough as nails and, eventually, unstoppable.

I'm rooting for you because we are in the same boat. Let's just make sure that boat ain't the Titanic!

Reach out to me on social media if you wanna chat or you just want to ask a question. I'm here to serve you with all of my life experiences!

You can do anything you want. Just try and never stop.

You're a superstar already.

—D.Y.

Email: dy@Deantèyoung.com
Twitter: @DeantèYoung
Instagram: @DeantèYoungBooks
Facebook:@mymanDeantè
LinkedIn: LinkedIn.com/in/Deantèyoung
Website: Deantèyoung.com

THE END